WE SHALL
OVERCOME

WE SHALL OVERCOME

HEROES OF THE
CIVIL RIGHTS MOVEMENT

FRED POWLEDGE

Photographs by the author

CHARLES SCRIBNER'S SONS · NEW YORK
Maxwell Macmillan Canada · Toronto
Maxwell Macmillan International
New York · Oxford · Singapore · Sydney

Text and photographs copyright © 1993 by Fred Powledge

Charles Scribner's Sons Books for Young Readers
Macmillan Publishing Company
866 Third Avenue, New York, NY 10022

Maxwell Macmillan Canada, Inc.
1200 Eglinton Avenue East, Suite 200
Don Mills, Ontario M3C 3N1

Macmillan Publishing Company is part of
the Maxwell Communication Group of Companies.

First edition   10 9 8 7 6 5 4 3 2 1
Printed in the United States of America

Library of Congress Cataloging-in-Publication Data
Powledge, Fred.
We shall overcome : heroes of the civil rights movement /
Fred Powledge. — 1st ed.   p.   cm.
Summary: Examines the system of segregation that existed in the United States until the mid-twentieth century and discusses the civil rights movement that changed this system.
ISBN 0-684-19362-0
1. Afro-Americans—Civil rights—Juvenile literature.
2. Civil rights movements—United States—History—20th century—Juvenile literature.
3. Civil rights workers—United States—Biography—Juvenile literature.
4. United States—Race relations—Juvenile literature.
[1. Afro-Americans—Civil rights.   2. Civil rights workers.
3. Civil rights movements.   4. United States—Race relations.]   I. Title.
E185.P68   1993   323.1'196073—dc20   92-25184

For all the people, black and white,
young and old,
who gave their lives for
the Movement

CONTENTS

CONTENTS

WE SHALL
OVERCOME

ONE

A Way of Life

Try to imagine a way of life in which you must be very careful about what you say, whom you say it to, the tone of voice you use, even the way you look at people. You have to be careful because you know that if you aren't, you can get into serious trouble. You know there are young people, people your own age, who were not careful enough, who briefly slipped and disobeyed the rules, and who were severely punished. Some of them were sent away to prison, and some even were seized from their homes at night and murdered.

You have to walk to school, sometimes great distances, because the school bus does not come for you, although it does pick up other people your age. In the fall, when you walk into the schoolroom to meet your new teacher, you can expect to receive old books, almost worn out and covered with the doodles and scrawls of other children you'll never know. In some places where farming is very important, you simply won't be going to school very much. The people who run things think it's more important that

1

you spend your time working in the fields—even if you're a child.

If you live in a city and you want to ride downtown, you have to sit at the rear of the bus. You cannot sit in the front part even if "your" section is full of people and the front is empty. In some places, you might have to hand the bus driver your money at the front door and then walk to the back door of the bus to get on. The front door is reserved for the other people. You could get arrested if you try to use it.

When you get downtown, if you want a drink of water, you have to get it out of a special water fountain reserved for people like you. When there is only one fountain, it is always for the *other* people, and you will be in trouble if you drink from it. If you are especially hot and thirsty and go into a store for a Coke, you will not be served a tall glass with lots of cracked ice and dark, sugary-tasting liquid like the other people. Nor will you be allowed to sit inside in the deliciously chilled air while you drink it. You will be handed a bottled drink, and you will be expected to go outside to drink it.

If you go with your mother into a department store, the store's employees will be happy to take her money for a new dress, but she cannot go into the fitting room to try it on. If you go with your father, you might hear people call him "Boy," even though he is a full-grown man. If you and he are walking down a narrow sidewalk and some of the other people approach, you and your father will be expected to step down into the gutter until the others have passed. Your mother and father will be expected to refer to the others as "Mr. So-and-so" and "Miss" and "Mrs.," but the others will call your parents and you, and even your grandparents, by only your first names.

A Way of Life

If you want to go to the movies, you might have to climb a rickety flight of outside stairs up to the balcony, a cramped and stuffy place where you and others like you are allowed to watch the show, while the other people (who pay the same money for tickets that you do) sit in more comfortable seats downstairs.

You are *discriminated against* by the other people and, it seems, by the whole world that lies outside your home and neighborhood. You know, or soon learn, that if you protest against this discrimination, your punishment can be quick and severe. A policeman may appear out of nowhere and take you down to the jail, or a social worker may come and snatch you away from your family. Or worse things might happen. You hear about these things even though your parents try, as parents always do, to shelter you from the scarier parts of life. The stories spread through your neighborhood almost as if they are carried on the night air: Charles (or William, or Bernard) has been in some sort of trouble. He said the wrong thing or was in the wrong place at the wrong time. He didn't lower his eyes when he was expected to, or he shot off his mouth. He heard that some people—the other people—had plans to do him harm. He left his home in a hurry and fled to another state or a faraway city. Or something far worse happened: A group of men came in the middle of the night and burst into his home and took him away. Nobody knows what happened to him, but everybody is afraid that he has been killed and dumped into the river.

It is terrifying. It is unfair. It is cruel. And it is crazy: There is no clear reason for things to be this way, and yet they are this way. And they show every sign of *staying* this way. It looks as if you will grow up and live your life the same way your parents lived theirs—minding your tongue,

3

lowering your eyes, hugging to yourself your thoughts of freedom from this oppressive way of life, being forced to accept second class in everything, participating in this terrible system even though you do not know why it exists.

Sometimes you wonder if *all* the other people are part of that system. You know there are people who are not outwardly mean to people like you. There are people who are polite, in a cool way (as if you were a stranger, although you live in the same small town together and you see each other frequently), or even friendly, or who show no feelings at all about the differences in the system. You wonder what *their* lives are like: What is it like to get a brand-new stack of schoolbooks in the fall, to sit on the ground floor at the movie house and see the screen from a different angle, to ride in the front of the bus, and to drink out of any water fountain you like. Most of all, you wonder what it must be like to not have to think about this system all the time. How must it be to not have to worry about being "different"?

The system, of course, was and is segregation. The people who were so badly mistreated were those whose skins were black, or brown, or tan. Back in the time when this system existed, which was not so long ago, the people were called Negroes (or, as the others sometimes put it, "colored people"). In more recent years, the descriptive terms *blacks* and *African-Americans* have been used, by others and by themselves. The people who operated the system were called Caucasians or whites (though their skin color was more pink than white). Not all the whites were part of the system. Some risked their lives to bring the system to an end.

4

A Way of Life

The system existed in the United States of America, and especially in the Southern states, in the 1960s. There are people alive today (and they are still *young* people, at least in their minds) who grew up under that system. There are people who are not yet fifty years old who came of age in a time of separate water fountains, raggedy schoolbooks, children picking cotton, and nighttime murders—and these are among the people who then smashed that terrible system to pieces.

These are the people who formed the civil rights movement. It was a movement that led to the creation of dozens of other freedom movements across the world. The struggles for women's liberation, gay rights, and freedom from political repression in Africa, China, and the Communist nations of Europe all can trace their origins back to the civil rights movement in the American South.

Sometimes, when these veterans of the Movement talk with young people today about the things that occurred under the system of segregation, the young people express amazement that it all happened. Today, it is difficult to imagine a situation in which water fountains and rest-room doors could have WHITE and COLORED signs on them, when you could be put in jail for going in the wrong door, and when you could be badly injured or even killed for something you said.

But it did happen. The system flourished for many years. It had the support of many of the leaders of Southern states, and they were able to get away with their behavior because, in addition to everything else, black people in many places were not allowed to vote. They could not help to throw the bad politicians out of office.

The system damaged many lives, both black and white,

5

and it was responsible for wasting enormous amounts of talent, skills, and money.

But now, although discrimination still exists in America and elsewhere, the basic system has been broken apart. No longer is discrimination encouraged or allowed by law in America. The separate water fountains are gone. Anybody can sit at the counter at any store that sells food to the public. Anybody who is old enough and meets a few basic requirements—and who is sufficiently concerned about his or her government—can vote.

It is a tribute to the people who destroyed the old system that it is so difficult to imagine those days now. In a fairly short number of years, a group of determined, dedicated people risked their lives to challenge the system. And they won. They are the heroes of the Movement.

TWO

Separate and Unequal

The heroes of the Movement had a long history behind them. It is a history that must be understood before the Movement itself, or the people who made it, can be fully appreciated. That history was based on the idea that one group of Americans must be kept separate from another.

The system of racial segregation in North America had its origins back in 1619, when the first black slaves were brought by ship to the Jamestown settlement in Virginia. There had been slavery elsewhere in the world for a long time before that, but these were America's first slaves. The twenty people with dark skin ("negars," they were called at the time)* were indentured servants—that is,

---

*Both history and language are forever changing, and that goes for the names by which black people have known themselves. For many years, the acceptable term for black people was *Negro*. It was the term used by themselves and by polite people of other races. Before the Movement started, *black* was not considered a very respectful term. But partly because of the success of the Movement, Negro Americans began to think of themselves in other, prouder ways, and the term *black* became not only acceptable, but (for many people) preferred.

after a certain period of working for their white "owners," they could receive a measure of freedom.

Indentured servant status, or servitude, was just one of several forms of slavery. All of them had one thing in common: Slavery was a way for one group of people (in this case, the whites) to take economic advantage of another (the blacks). There was work to be done in establishing the new country. Slavery was a way to get someone to do that work without spending much money. It was also a way to get the most backbreaking work done by someone else—the clearing of land, the digging of irrigation ditches, the stoop labor of cultivating and picking cotton and tobacco.

The leaders of the European world supported slavery. Countries that often are thought of as "advanced" and as shining examples of "civilization" apparently saw little wrong with snatching people from their ancestral homes (sometimes splitting up families in the process), packing them like sardines into ships, and transporting them across oceans to be sold at public auction. Most of this theft of human life took place in Africa. Nobody knows how many people were uprooted and sent to foreign lands. One estimate is that fifteen million slaves arrived alive in America. Many others died on the horrible voyage. Historians think that more than fifty million people were torn from their African homes and shackled with the chains of slavery.

In more recent years, some blacks have expressed preferences for other terms, such as *African-American* or *Afro-American*, and an older term, *person of color*, seems to be making a comeback. In this book, no one term is given precedence over another, although there is an attempt to use the expression that was in most common use at the time—*Negro* in the 1950s and early 1960s, for example, and *black* later on.

Angry reaction against the system began almost immediately. That is an important thing to remember when one studies social revolutions of this sort, whether they be the civil rights movement of the 1960s or the struggles today of people to improve their lives in places all around the world. Whenever there has been repression, whether it has been the bondage of slavery or the indignity of separate water fountains, there have been equally strong efforts to defeat that repression. People, it seems, just do not take well to being pushed around and exploited. Sooner or later, they fight back.

In the case of slavery, black men and women sometimes ran away from their cruel masters, seeking safety in parts of the nation where slavery was not tolerated. Sometimes they rebelled directly, letting their "owners" know in no uncertain terms that they would take harsh treatment no longer. In the case of the civil rights movement of thirty years ago, there was very little running away. Blacks stayed and rebelled, and they even managed to do so without returning the violence that so often was directed at them.

It is important to remember, also, that throughout the centuries since the first slaves arrived in America, and continuing right up to today, it has been economic power—money—that has been at the base of the unfair system. Slavery, and the system of racial segregation that followed it, were convenient ways for some people to benefit financially from the work of others. Even the highest courts in the nation gave support to the idea. In 1857, the Supreme Court of the United States declared that Negroes were not citizens. Little time was lost in translating this ruling into economic terms: Since black people could not be citizens, the federal government reasoned, they didn't qualify for the free land grants that were being handed out in the West to families and individuals. Noncitizenship for Negroes didn't work both ways, however; black people were supposed to pay taxes, just like whites, and they'd get into trouble if they didn't.

In 1861, as the Civil War began between Northern and Southern states, the new constitution written by the leadership of the Confederacy in Alabama declared that, for purposes of representation and taxation, slaves were equivalent to three-fifths of a person. It was a chilling thought: that you, because of the color of your skin, were worth only three-fifths as much as that other human being. Slavery, said the Confederacy, "is a natural and normal condition."

The Civil War wasn't fought strictly over slavery (there were other financial issues as well, such as the unequal costs of shipping agricultural products between the North and South). But one of the results of the South's defeat was the end of slavery in the United States. The change was reflected, as might be expected, in the market price of humans: In 1861, at the war's start, a twenty-year-old male slave sold for as much as $1,050; four years later, the price was $100. (The leadership of the North thought in economic terms, too; it welcomed blacks in the fight against the South in the Civil War, but they were given low-ranking jobs and were paid poorly. The navy, for example, enlisted Negroes, but said they could rise no higher in rank than "boys" and paid them $10 a month and one meal a day. Blacks have always been discriminated against in the North, as well as in the South.)

After the Civil War and the formal end of slavery, America seemed like a place that was uncertain of its true feelings about the dark-skinned people who made up 13 percent of its population. On the one hand, there were political speeches and legislation that appeared to welcome the black person, finally, into the American community. But on the other hand, there was discrimination that rivaled that of slavery days. On the plus side, in 1866, one year after the war ended, Congress passed civil rights legislation that extended citizenship to "all persons born in the United States and not subject to any foreign powers, excluding Indians not taxed." Americans of "every race and color" could sign contracts, buy and sell property, and go into court to settle their grievances. Two years later, the nation accepted the Fourteenth Amendment to the Constitution, which says that no state shall "deny to any person within its jurisdiction the equal protection of the laws." That term—*equal protection of the laws*—has been used since then in countless court decisions, some of them extremely important, as a declaration that racial (and other forms of) discrimination are illegal in America.

But thirty years later, a Supreme Court decision put another spin on the term *equal protection*. In a case named *Plessy* v. *Ferguson*, the court said it was "reasonable" for states to provide "separate but equal" facilities for Negroes. It was legal, then, for a state (most were in the South, but not all) to establish separate schools for whites and blacks, as long as it could be effectively argued that the schools were "equal."

The decision seemed to reflect a feeling in white America that has existed for a long time, and that unfortunately lives even today: In the minds of some whites, there is something "wrong" with blacks and the two races should exist separately. "Separate but equal" was a way of saying separation and segregation are all right because all the facilities are the same for both races—the quality of schools, seats on city buses, justice in the courtroom.

It was a foolish argument. For one thing, it's simply a waste of time, money, talent, and other resources to expect two groups of people to exist within the same society but *separately*. The amount of money spent on plumbing alone—for two sets of water fountains, two sets of rest rooms—is a tremendous waste.

Second, it was (and is) irrational to expect that "separate" really would be "equal." "Separate but equal" may have been one thing in theory, but in the real world it meant that the people in charge built better schools for white children (and sent the whites' cast-off textbooks to the black children). They paved the streets in front of white residents' homes and left mud and dust in the black neighborhoods. They gave blacks less chance of getting justice in a courtroom or when they were stopped for speeding by a white police officer.

People who opposed segregation understood very clearly the absurdity of this thinking, and they challenged "separate but equal" in federal court. In several of the cases, Negroes who had been denied admission to schools of higher education—law schools, particularly—went to court to argue that their rights were being violated. After a black graduate student in education won such a case in the late 1940s against the University of Oklahoma, the school let him in. But it forced him to sit apart from the other students when he ate his meals in the cafeteria and when he read books in the library. When he went to class, he had to sit in a separate classroom that was next door to the one where his fellow students listened to their teacher. He heard what was going on through an open door between the two rooms. In another celebrated case, *Sweatt* v. *Painter*, the University of Texas had wanted so badly to keep Heman M. Sweatt, a black man, out of its law school that it had created a separate *black school*! The Supreme Court ordered the university to admit Sweatt to the "white" school in 1950, but the Court's ruling managed to avoid throwing out the separate-but-equal idea.

All this time, black Americans and whites who opposed segregation were challenging it in other ways. In 1941, as America was entering World War II, the country needed thousands of employees in industries that were building the materials of war—tanks, guns, airplanes. A. Philip Randolph saw an opportunity to strike a blow for equality in the workplace. Randolph was the founder of the Brotherhood of Sleeping Car Porters, the labor union that represented Negro railroad employees, and he was a lifelong fighter for equality.

The labor leader sent word to President Franklin D. Roosevelt that unless blacks got equal treatment, he would lead a huge march to Washington. He knew that such a march would be terribly embarrassing to Roosevelt, not only because it would raise questions about the leader's own commitment to equality, but also because the president's wife, Eleanor Roosevelt, was well known for her commitment to ending discrimination. The president quickly signed an executive order that outlawed discrimination in government and defense employment. Randolph called off the march.

In 1942, a group of blacks and whites in Chicago formed an organization called the Congress of Racial Equality, or CORE. The group held sit-in strikes at restaurants that refused to allow blacks to enter. The sit-in was a technique that was borrowed from the labor movement. It consisted of walking into a place and politely but firmly sitting down. In the case of restaurants, it was a way of saying, "I'm sitting here until you decide to serve me." The technique was simple, and it was effective; it got the attention of the press and the other customers, and it did so without violence—at least on the part of the demonstrators. Sometimes, those who were against the sit-in would jostle or dump food on the demonstrators, but that seemed only to make the sit-inners look better.

Negroes who were fed up with being discriminated against on public transportation started thinking of ways to change the situation. One simple and obvious approach would be to walk instead of ride. City buses in the South made much of their money from black riders, even though the bus companies treated blacks like second-class citizens. Baton Rouge, Louisiana, was one of those places. In 1953, the fares paid by black customers accounted for an estimated two-thirds of the bus company's income. When the "colored" section was filled on one of Baton Rouge's buses, Negroes had to stand in the aisles even if there was room in the "white" section. When the city refused to change the system, black riders started a boycott that was remarkably effective. In the end, the blacks' leaders and the city reached a compromise and the boycott ended.

At the same time, efforts were being made to insure that the Negro had equal rights at the one place that could do the most to change the system: the ballot box. Those who favored segregation, particularly in the South, had devised a complicated set of rules to make sure that, first of all, blacks would find it too difficult to register as voters. If they didn't register, they couldn't cast their votes on election day, and the system would continue as before. Second, those who made the rules saw to it that blacks who *did* manage to make it through the registration maze would have votes that had little weight. An elaborate set of party primaries and runoff elections made sure that this was the case. Slowly but surely, Negroes challenged this system and won victories against it in the federal courts.

Enforcing those victories proved to be much harder than winning them. Once the segregationists saw their discriminatory laws struck down, they used economic pressure, violence, and threats of violence against black citizens who expressed a desire to register and vote. A black man who worked for the county highway department might lose his job if he registered to vote; black women who were schoolteachers—even those who taught their students about being good citizens and taking part in the democratic process—might find themselves suddenly out of work if they tried to take part in that process themselves.

And all the time, the system that was segregation became stronger and stronger. The builders and backers of the system were constantly on guard against attempts to challenge it. Police officers were harsh and sometimes brutal with those who questioned authority. In 1959, when a black student applied at a "white" college in Mississippi, the governor had him sent to a mental institution. Sometimes those who spoke out—black and white—would find themselves in jail, facing charges based on false, made-up evidence. Courageous black lawyers in the Deep South were called "boy" and denied even the right to sit down when they appeared in court to defend their clients. The federal court system was the closest thing a black person had to a friend in court, but even some federal judges were racists. One of them, who was appointed to the court in Mississippi in 1961, even compared Negroes to chimpanzees.

But the opposition to that system became stronger and stronger, too. At the center of the opposition was a group of hardworking black attorneys, many of them graduates of the law school at Howard University, a highly rated, predominantly black school in Washington, D.C. The lawyers, and those who worked with them, thought their best attack on segregation would be through the schoolhouse door. They hoped that once discrimination ended in education, it would be easier to vanquish in other areas of life.

Education had always been important to Negroes in America, just as it has been to all groups of people who have come to these shores—even when they came voluntarily, not in chains. Negroes believed that a good education is a way to get not only out of ignorance but also out of poverty—and, especially, out of discrimination. It was a way to achieve full citizenship, even in a nation that did not want Negroes to have full citizenship.

The famous Negro educator Booker T. Washington made a speech in Atlanta in 1895 in which he advised blacks to set aside thoughts of integration and equality and concentrate instead on becoming independent through education. Washington said, in a line that has been quoted many times since: "In all things that are purely social we can be as separate as the fingers, yet one as the hand in all things essential to mutual progress." Washington's speech was mocked by some blacks as a sellout to the segregationists, and it was applauded by whites who did not want segregation to end. But what he said about the importance of education stuck with many black Americans. To get ahead and to become independent of the system, he was saying, you've got to educate yourself. It's a formula that millions of Americans of all colors and ethnic backgrounds have followed, and for good reason: It works.

The black lawyers' attacks on segregated education came to a head in the legal case that is known, for short, as *Brown* v. *Board of Education*. The case concerned separate schools in Topeka, Kansas, but by the time the Supreme Court heard it, it was combined with similar cases from South Carolina, Delaware, and Virginia. In each place, black children had been denied the right to attend "white" schools. They had been told to attend their own black schools. On May 17, 1954, the chief justice of the Supreme Court, Earl Warren, delivered the Court's unanimous decision. It was simple and momentous. For many people it represented the beginning of the civil rights movement.

The Court said that "separate but equal" was no longer legal. If a school system was separate, it was by definition unequal. Chief Justice Warren wrote: "We conclude that in the field of public education the doctrine of 'separate but equal' has no place. Separate educational facilities are inherently unequal." The black children were being denied their right of equal protection of the law, said the court—the right that is guaranteed by the Fourteenth Amendment to the Constitution. The old rule established by *Plessy* v. *Ferguson* was no longer in effect.

A new and more exciting era in the struggle for equality began. For the first time, the government of the United States was saying that segregation is wrong and it must be changed. The decision brought new hope and strength to Negroes and whites who had been working for equality all along. It also brought anger and desperation to many segregationists, who feared that their system was being attacked, that perhaps it might be in danger of disappearing completely. These segregationists fought back more fiercely than ever before, using all the power at their command to pass state laws, to bring economic pressure against black people, and to use violence against those who dared to speak out. These methods had, to some extent, succeeded before, whenever the segregated system was under challenge. But this time things were different. A new movement was being born, the new Supreme Court ruling had given it new strength, and a new generation of heroes was coming along to make it victorious.

THREE

Marchin' Shoes

The Supreme Court's *Brown* decision brought new waves of excited hope to the hearts of many black Americans, as well as to whites who agreed with them that segregation was wrong and that segregation in education was especially cruel. A lot of people thought that it was only a short time before segregation would be vanquished from America.

Many of the black people who today are veterans of the civil rights movement say that they assumed that once the highest court in the land had spoken, the change from a segregated society would take place with ease. Sure, there would be some grumbling from the die-hard segregationists, and there would be outright opposition in the states where segregation had traditionally been strongest, but the *Brown* decision was the law of the land, and it would have to be followed.

They were wrong. The political leaders of the South—the governors and the legislatures—clung tightly to the old system of segregation, somehow hoping that a decision from the Supreme Court, even a unanimous one, would not bring any change. For years, they were right. But eventually the system crumbled.

There were several reasons for the slow pace at which school desegregation took place. One of them had to do with the Supreme Court itself. When it delivered its momentous 1954 decision, the court did not set a specific time by which the separate-but-equal schools had to be converted into one system, open to children of all colors and races. Instead, the court said it wanted to hear further suggestions from the interested parties on how best its ruling could be carried out. The interested parties included, of course, the lawyers for the black children who had been denied equal education. But they also included representatives of the very states that had denied blacks that equality.

Some of the formerly segregated states studied the court's decision and immediately proceeded to end segregation in the classroom. They included school districts in Arizona, Arkansas, Delaware, Kansas, Maryland, Missouri, New Mexico, and West Virginia. These states, along with Texas and Kentucky, are sometimes referred to as border states, to distinguish them from the states of the Deep South, which included Louisiana, Mississippi, Alabama, Georgia, Florida, and South Carolina, and those of the upper South, which included North Carolina, Tennessee, and Virginia.

In some places, the political leadership did more than it was legally required to do. Atlanta was one such place. It was the capital of a strictly segregationist Georgia, but Atlanta's leaders wanted their city to maintain its reputation as a forward-thinking place. That would be necessary, they knew, if they were to attract high-quality businesses. So Atlanta desegregated all its public recreation centers in 1954 (although it waited several years to desegregate its schools).

That was certainly not the case in the deepest South. Leaders of those states used the Supreme Court's hesitation over implementing the *Brown* decision to delay actual desegregation as much as they could. (There was sometimes a bit of confusion over the terms *desegregation* and *integration*. To most of those who were involved with the process in the fifties and sixties, *desegregation* meant simply the end of segregation. An example might be the quiet announcement that a city-run skating rink or golf course or elementary school would no longer be operated in a segregated manner. *Integration* meant desegregation and then some; not only would the barriers be lowered, but a real effort would be made to bring Negroes in to facilities that formerly had been all white. A white school could be desegregated—that is, in theory open to all—without actually having any black pupils. For it to be integrated, the school board would need to establish rules assuring that both black and white students attended—for example, requiring that school buses bring pupils from both black and white neighborhoods. For much of the deepest South, however, there were no plans for either desegregation or integration.)

You might wonder why the white leaders of places such as Alabama, Mississippi, Louisiana, Georgia, South Carolina, North Carolina, and Virginia thought delay would accomplish anything worthwhile. Wouldn't it be better to just get it over with—to follow the law of the land and get on with life? Furthermore, wasn't it the right thing to do?

The answer was simple, say some of those white leaders

nowadays, when they reflect on the events of the 1950s: They wanted to keep on getting elected. They feared that if they went along with the Court's decision and desegregated the schools, the voters would angrily turn them out of office. "The voters," in this case, did not include any significant number of Negro citizens, who might have wanted to *reward* the politicians for their courageous actions. Very few Negroes were allowed to vote in the segregated states.

The white politicians' attempts at delaying desegregation might have been insignificant if the federal government had shown more backbone in ordering an end to segregated schooling. But it didn't. After its May 17 decision, the Supreme Court seemed to think of desegregation as a burden on white Americans (and to ignore the great burden that *segregation* had always been on black Americans); the Court gave the segregated states plenty of time to carry out the change. The Court asked the South to draw up plans for desegregating the schools "with all deliberate speed." That term may have sounded like an order to start the change immediately, but to the segregationists it was an open invitation to drag things out as long as they could. They accepted the invitation gladly. They used the time to build massive political and economic walls against the time when desegregation would finally come. No one knows how the course of history would have been changed if the Southern states had simply followed the Supreme Court's ruling and concentrated on providing the best schools—and lives—for all their citizens.

Desegregation might also have moved faster if the political leadership at the national level had acted more firmly. This indecisiveness could be seen in the reaction of President Dwight D. Eisenhower to the planned desegregation of a public high school in Little Rock, Arkansas. The Little Rock school board had drawn up a plan for desegregating the school in the fall of 1957. On the night before nine Negroes were scheduled to walk through the doors of Central High School, the governor of Arkansas, Orval Faubus, threw a monkey wrench into the plans. He sent the state National Guard to Little Rock to "preserve order," although the only disorder was caused by wild statements from the governor himself. Eventually those statements drew a mob of angry whites to the school. The violent mob and the National Guard—and Faubus's inflammatory talk—kept the students from entering the school. Finally, President Eisenhower sent in federal troops to keep the peace, but by then the segregationists knew that they had the upper hand. Eventually, Faubus closed the school, and Little Rock students were deprived of an education for an entire school year.

Time and again in the years that followed, the leadership in Washington showed its reluctance to demonstrate that it truly wanted segregation to end. And time and again, the segregationists seized on this reluctance to delay the moment that any thinking person knew would finally come.

There was another kind of leadership, though, that was *not* reluctant to act. In fact, events such as the Supreme Court's *Brown* decision had made this leadership bolder and stronger than ever before. This was the leadership that had existed all along in the black community. White society hardly knew it was there. But it was, and it was active and powerful. This leadership was not a single man or woman who spoke for all the people in the community; rather, it was a network of all sorts of people who were fed up with segregation and who were determined to finally do something about it.

The network included officials and members of organizations that had been fighting for equality for decades. Number one among these was the National Association for the Advancement of Colored People, or NAACP. The network also usually included people in the black community who were financially independent of white society. These were the funeral home operators, lawyers, presidents of private colleges, and owners of businesses that operated only in black neighborhoods. Very often the leadership included Negro railroad workers, members of A. Philip Randolph's Brotherhood of Sleeping Car Porters. These workers travelled frequently among the different regions of the country, and they brought to the South news of what life was like out there in the rest of America. They also brought copies of Negro newspapers and magazines that were published in the North and portrayed black people in positive ways. (All too often, when a black person was mentioned in a local newspaper in the South, it was in an account of a crime. Local newspapers prided themselves on printing news of interest to the community—births, deaths, and weddings—but almost without exception the items concerned only white people. In some of the South's larger cities, including Atlanta and Birmingham, Alabama, blacks published their own newspapers.)

The leadership almost always included ministers from Negro churches, especially the Baptist and Methodist faiths. Since the days of slavery, the church had been an important force in black Americans' lives. It offered hope that conditions would change for the better someday. Perhaps just as importantly, it offered Negroes a place where they could go—on Sunday morning or any other time—and be free of the insults that normally were heaped upon them by a segregated society. The black church offered exciting, emotional preaching, and it offered passionate singing of hymns that gave people hope for a better existence.

Black people had used some of those songs since slavery days to say things that they otherwise could not say, for fear that their white masters would hear them. When they were concealed in a song, the words sometimes had more than one meaning. Thus they formed an effective code language. When someone sang that she was going to "cross the River Jordan" and "get my freedom on the other side," she may have been talking about someday entering the blessed land of heaven, where hatred and discrimination were not known—or she may have been letting her friends know that she planned to wade across the river tonight and strike out for a part of the country where slavery was outlawed. *Or* she may have just been expressing the feeling that someday she would leave this place. Like any good music of today, these songs served many purposes and were important means of communication.

Once the civil rights movement became a powerful force in the nation in the 1960s, many church songs were informally converted to "freedom songs," sometimes with words that had been slightly changed to fit the occasion. The powerful music filled the churches that served as the Movement's major meeting places, and the songs filled the singers with courage and determination to march out the door across the paved "River Jordan" that divided black and white neighborhoods, and then down the street to lodge their protests with city hall or the county courthouse. That courage and that determination were important because what often awaited the marchers downtown was arrest, and sometimes a beating.

And the leadership of the black community included ordinary people. Or at least they *seemed* ordinary until they went into action. That's the way it often is with leadership: People whom you might expect would be lifetime followers are sometimes thrust into situations that demand intelligent action, and they become leaders.

All of these various components of leadership had come together in Montgomery, Alabama, on December 1, 1955, in what would be known as the Montgomery bus boycott.

It started when Rosa Parks, a black woman who was an assistant tailor at a Montgomery department store and an active member and officer of the local NAACP chapter, defied the order of a city bus driver to give up her seat to a white man. Some versions of the story depict Parks as someone whose feet were "just tired" after a hard day's work, but the truth is that her soul had been achingly tired of segregation for quite some time. Rosa Parks had challenged the seating rules before and had once been forced to leave a bus. She also had helped plan attempts by black NAACP members to borrow books from the city's "white" library. (They had been unsuccessful.)

This time, Parks defied Montgomery's law that reserved the first ten rows of bus seats for whites. Like many of the South's segregation laws and customs, this one was complicated. If the black section was full, even if there were no whites on the bus, Negroes could not sit in those front rows; they had to stand in the back. And if white people filled up their section, blacks would have to move from their section—a row at a time, starting in the front—to make room for whites.

Rosa Parks and other Negroes were occupying seats in the front row of the black section. The white section filled up, and a white man was left standing. The bus driver ordered the Negroes to move from row eleven to make room for the one white man. Everybody but Rosa Parks moved. The driver called the police and had her arrested.

Word of her arrest spread quickly through the black community. The black leadership in Montgomery had been planning a challenge to segregation in that Alabama city, and the arrest seemed to be the perfect starting point. An organization was quickly formed. It was called the Montgomery Improvement Association, and a young minister who had come to town less than two years before was chosen to head it. His name was Martin Luther King, Jr.

The Reverend Dr. Martin Luther King, Jr., was the son of a prominent Atlanta family. His father and his grandfather had been ministers, and the young minister had received an excellent education at Morehouse College in Atlanta and at Boston University. It soon became apparent that he was far more than a talented Baptist minister with a lot of book-learning. Dr. King quickly showed that he had a special sort of leadership that appealed to people from all stations of life, whether they were well educated or not educated at all, whether they were financially comfortable or struggling to make ends meet. His speaking style was especially moving. And when he preached about the evils of segregation and the need for black people and white people of good conscience to come together to put an end to the system, he inspired great courage in the hearts of those who heard him.

In the years that followed the Montgomery bus boycott, when Dr. King became the most celebrated leader of the Movement, even some of those whites who opposed change the most found themselves showing respect for this man. Martin Luther King, Jr., was not just a politician, saying what he thought the public wanted to hear. It was obvious that he believed deeply in what he said. And one of the things he said, over and over again in that rhythmic beat of the Southern black preacher, was, "Put on your marchin' shoes, children." And over and over again, people did just that, and they marched with Dr. King down to the courthouses and the city halls of the South and made their "witness" for freedom. What's more, they did all this nonviolently.

Dr. King was a believer in the methods of Mohandas K. Gandhi, who had used nonviolence in India in the 1920s and 1930s to lead an independence movement against Great Britain. Dr. King, and others in the American movement, believed that no matter how much violence the other side inflicted on those who worked for equality, the members of the Movement should not strike back.

For many Movement people, this rule was based on religion, and specifically on the Bible's precept that "whosoever shall smite thee on thy right cheek, turn to him the other also." There were others in the Movement who did not share this religious conviction, but they did see that nonviolence was an effective tool to use against the opposition, which was often violent. America likes to talk about its belief in fair play, and it clearly was not fair play when a howling white mob beat nonviolent men and women, and even children, with clubs and sticks. Scenes such as this, which many Americans saw in newspaper photographs and on television, helped convince even some of those who favored segregation that violence was not the solution to their race relations problems.

The Montgomery boycott was a victory for the black community. People who had used the city buses to get to work and to do their shopping stopped riding them, and the bus company's income fell dramatically. As had been the case in Baton Rouge in 1953, black people shared rides and walked rather than take the bus. Negro churches became the meeting places for the boycotters and the collection points for the ride-sharing program. They also served as the places where boycotters could keep warm during the cold winter of 1955–1956. There were taxicab companies in Montgomery that were owned by black people, and these cabs offered to carry riders at cut rates—the same prices the buses had been charging. When city officials heard about this practice, they used pressure to make the cab companies charge their usual rates. Attempts such as this to force the boycott to end did no good, however, and a little more than a year after it had started, the boycotters won a victory. They reached an agreement with the city that favored the protestors. Not long afterward, however, in 1957, the segregationists showed their anger by firing shots into Dr. King's home and setting off bombs at four black churches and in the homes of two ministers, one Negro and one white, who had favored desegregation. The violence was part of a pattern that would develop as the

Movement grew: After almost every victory for the anti-segregation forces, bombs or gunfire would remind everyone that the battle was not yet over. Only rarely did the police catch the people responsible for these acts of violence. In far too many parts of the South, the police and the rest of the justice system were clearly on the side of the segregationists, even those who used violence.

One of the most important outcomes of the Montgomery boycott was that it served as a model and an inspiration for Negroes elsewhere in the South and the nation, and even the world. Montgomery was a strictly segregated city, and it was in one of the most segregated states in the Deep South. If black people could rebel against segregation in Alabama, they could do it anywhere.

Martin Luther King, Jr., and other leaders, most of them black ministers from the South, formed a new organization in 1957 that was dedicated to fighting racism. They named it the Southern Christian Leadership Conference (SCLC). The choice of the words in the name was significant. *Christian* was there because most of the group's members were Baptist preachers. It also reflected the turn-the-other-cheek philosophy of nonviolence. And the group's founders were careful to demonstrate their feelings about the Movement's positive contributions to society by choosing the word *leadership*.

The Montgomery bus boycott also helped bring pressure on Congress to pass the Civil Rights Act of 1957, one of several such laws that would be enacted in the Movement years. The act made it somewhat easier for Negroes to register and vote, and it gave civil rights a higher priority at the federal level, particularly in the U.S. Department of Justice, the federal agency that is supposed to enforce civil rights laws.

The bus boycott also showed that black people, when confronted with an obstacle, could stick together and overcome it. For a long time, segregationists had kept black people down and powerless by dividing them and encouraging them to distrust one another. The boycott in Montgomery showed that this technique would work no longer. It also demonstrated to a lot of young black people that organization and protest worked. These young people had already seen, in the *Brown* school decision, that the national leadership in Washington felt segregation and the idea of "separate but equal" was against the law (at least in education). Now they were seeing what could happen if black people went out on their own and defied racism head-on.

As Negro militancy increased, so did violence against black people, including some to those who had never been part of any movement at all. In 1955, shortly before the Montgomery boycott started, there were three incidents of lynching in Mississippi. Lynching is the killing of someone without legal authority. It has been used against all sorts of people, black and white, but in these years it almost always referred to the gruesome murders of Negroes. The Reverend George W. Lee was murdered because he was leading a voter registration drive. Lamar Smith was lynched in Brookhaven, and a fourteen-year-old black boy was lynched in Leflore County. It was the boy's lynching that struck the nerve of the nation.

The boy was named Emmett Till. He had been visiting relatives in Mississippi, and it was said that he had whistled at a white woman in a store. The lynchers beat and killed Till and mutilated his body. When his body was returned to Chicago, his mother made the heroic decision to leave her child's casket open. Millions of Americans—in person in Chicago or through photographs in newspapers and magazines—saw Emmett Till's savagely beaten face. Throughout the nation today, you can find people who trace their involvement in the civil rights movement to the moment they saw that photo or heard about Emmett Till. The awful crime helped them decide on a life of fighting segregation and racism.

Four years later, another lynching shocked the world and angered Americans. A young Negro named Mack Charles Parker, who had been accused of raping a white woman, was taken from his jail cell in Poplarville, Mississippi, by a white mob. He was beaten and murdered, and his body was dumped into the Pearl River. The white state authorities did nothing about the crime. That was the pattern in much of the South, where there were not only two sets of water fountains but two distinct forms of justice.

The legislatures of the Southern states did little to confront this sort of violence, and in some ways they promoted it. They scurried about, passing laws that (they told the white voters) would insure that desegregation would "never happen here." At the same time, their members secretly knew that what they were doing was only stalling. The more knowledgeable of them knew, too, that there had been a very important change in the black community: Black people could no longer be ignored or treated like children. The anger at segregation had been there all along, of course, ever since the first slave ships arrived.

But it had gained nourishment from the Supreme Court decision in 1954, had been given a giant boost with the Montgomery bus boycott of 1955, and was turned into a holy crusade with the lynching that year of Emmett Till. The civil rights movement was gathering its strength, and soon it would become a surging tide.

Then came February 1, 1960. A handful of neatly dressed black college students sat down at a lunch counter in a Woolworth's five-and-ten-cent store in downtown Greensboro, North Carolina, and the tide became a huge, unstoppable wave that washed across the South, the nation, and the world.

FOUR

The Power of Nonviolence

The sit-in that took place in Greensboro on that February morning was no more an accident than the Montgomery bus boycott had been. The Greensboro demonstration may have been a surprise for most members of the *white* community, but the college students and their elders had been planning it for some time. Their counterparts who attended black colleges in Nashville, Tennessee, were about to start similar protests.

As we have seen, the North Carolina sit-in was not the first such demonstration. But it was the first such demonstration in the South since the Supreme Court's *Brown* decision had focussed so much attention on civil rights and race relations.

The four young men were freshmen at North Carolina Agricultural and Technical College (known as A&T) in Greensboro. On February 1, after weeks of talking about what sort of demonstration they wanted to hold, they walked into the Woolworth's store in downtown Greensboro and bought a few small items. Then they strolled over to the store's lunch counter and sat down. One of them, Ezell Blair, Jr., asked for a cup of coffee.

The waitress replied with the words that would soon become familiar to many a black person in the South and elsewhere: "I'm sorry. We don't serve Negroes here." One of the students politely mentioned that the store *had* been willing to take their money earlier, when they had been purchasing merchandise. The waitress told the students they could get served at the other end of the counter, in a section without stools where people could buy food to take out. Segregation at this lunch counter, and at many other places, seemed controlled by a crazy rule: If you're standing up, it's okay; if you want to sit down, go away.

The students stood their ground—or rather they *sat* their ground. In addition to Ezell Blair, Jr., they were David Richmond, Franklin McCain, and Joseph McNeil. Eventually the store closed and they left. They and other students returned the next day to continue the protest. A newspaper photograph taken then showed the students, most of them wearing neckties and jackets, sitting at the counter and doing their homework while they waited for the store to change its policy. Signs nearby showed that a turkey club sandwich cost sixty-five cents, and a hot dog cost twenty cents. But you could not sit down to eat either one in this store if you weren't white.

Day after day, the store allowed the students to return and sit at the counter, but it didn't serve them any food. Curious people, black and white, came to see what was happening, and the press got interested in the story. The *real* interest, however, was on the campuses of black colleges and universities, and even some high schools, throughout the South.

The students quickly recognized that this was a way they could take part in the struggle to end segregation. (Not many people referred to it as "the Movement" then, but that was certainly what it was rapidly becoming.) Many of the young people thought, as young people always think, that their elders—their parents, ministers, teachers, and other community leaders—weren't moving fast enough. They wanted to take advantage of the tremendous push given to the struggle by events such as the *Brown* decision and the Montgomery boycott. They wanted results *now*. Sitting in was something that young people could be good at. The elders could continue with their own methods— negotiating with the white "power structures" that ran local government, bringing legal action (as they had done in *Brown*)—when negotiations failed. Ezell Blair, Jr., explained to a reporter in 1960 how the students felt when he said black adults "have been complacent and fearful. It is time for someone to wake up and change the situation, and we decided to start here."

What if the students were arrested? What if violent white people came out of the crowd of onlookers and attacked the sit-inners? The students considered these possibilities, but they didn't spend a lot of time worrying about what might happen. Traditionally, it is not until people get older and have more responsibilities on their shoulders that they start worrying about such likelihoods. The students' parents worried a great deal about them, however.

One by one, student groups elsewhere in the South held their own sit-ins. The young people at Nashville's black colleges started their demonstrations almost immediately. Usually the protests were held at variety stores, like the one in Greensboro, that were happy to accept Negroes' money for purchases of merchandise but refused to serve them equally at their lunch counters. These stores were almost always downtown. Much of their business came from black people who rode buses from their homes on the black side of town to work in the white community. Often the transfer points for the bus lines were in the center of town; they provided the variety stores with a large supply of potential customers. Some of these stores, like Woolworth's, were parts of nationwide chains. While their outlets in Northern cities did not have segregated facilities, the stores in the North were picketed by black and white citizens who carried signs in sympathy for the Southerners. The picketing put the stores under tremendous pressure because it cost them sales and made them look bigoted. Some of their executives actually wanted to desegregate and get it over with, but local laws and local politics required that they remain segregated in the South. In those days, the downtown areas of many Southern cities were served by one or more locally owned department stores, and these businesses, too, were the targets of demonstrators.

The white South's reaction to the sit-ins was varied. In several places, legislators and city council members hurriedly passed laws declaring the students' actions illegal. These laws were ruled unconstitutional by the time they were tested in the federal courts, but in the meantime many students were hauled off to jail, charged with "trespassing" or "disorderly conduct" and "parading without a permit." They usually were released quickly because the jails became overcrowded and because local officials had problems explaining why they were treating such polite people like suspected criminals.

In some places, especially in the border states, groups

of local business and political leaders immediately started trying to work out agreements that would end the protests and provide a measure of desegregation. They wanted to remove the spotlight of public attention that was shining on them. Some places desegregated quietly. In others, white troublemakers *did* come out of the crowd and bully and sometimes punch the well-mannered students. One favorite technique of the bullies was to dump a bottle of ketchup or a bowl of sugar, or both, on the students.

The students hardly ever fought back. They knew the value of nonviolence. They knew that if it were used correctly, nonviolence could be a mightier weapon than all the punches—or even guns—that might be aimed at them. They knew that by not fighting back, they were showing that they were morally superior to those who tormented them. And they knew that they were winning supporters by their calm, strong behavior. The Nashville group was particularly skilled in its understanding and use of nonviolence. The Nashvillians say that one of the reasons the sit-ins started in Greensboro rather than in the Tennessee city is that the Nashville students spent far more time studying and practicing nonviolence, making sure that when the time came to demonstrate, they would be mentally and physically ready for whatever might happen.

The leader of these workshops was a young black divinity student named James Lawson, a pacifist who had gone to prison rather than serve in the military during the Korean War, which lasted from 1950 to 1953.

In some of Lawson's workshops, the students took turns pretending to be white bullies who poured verbal and physical abuse on the students who were playing the parts of sit-inners. They knew this practice would make them ready for the real thing when it happened. Staff members of the Congress of Racial Equality, who had held their own sit-ins back in the 1940s, went to the South and held nonviolence workshops of their own. They, too, used play-acting to get young people ready for anything that might happen and to train them in the art of not fighting back.

The activists also discussed another important question that was to be asked many times during the Movement years: How could they be in favor of breaking one law (the one requiring segregation at lunch counters, for example) when they were also in favor of supporting another (the Supreme Court's school decision, for example)?

One reply was to come a few years later from Martin Luther King, Jr., in his famous 1963 "Letter from Birmingham Jail," which was addressed to white clergymen who had been critical of his techniques. There were, wrote Dr. King, "two types of laws: just and unjust." People had a moral responsibility to obey the just laws. People also had a moral responsibility to *disobey* unjust laws. How to tell the difference between the two? Dr. King's answer was: "A just law is a man-made code that squares with the moral law or the law of God. An unjust law is a code that is out of harmony with the moral law."

Nine weeks after the Greensboro sit-ins started, colleges and universities throughout the nation closed briefly for the annual Easter vacation. Some students, those from the more social-minded white colleges, headed to Florida for the annual event that is called spring break. But the local leaders of the student protest movement went to Raleigh, North Carolina, to the campus of Shaw University, to discuss the movement they were creating. Ella Baker, the executive director of the Southern Christian

Leadership Conference and a long-time NAACP worker for equality in the South and the nation, recognized the importance of the sit-ins and saw the need for its leaders to get together and compare notes on their activities. Baker expected a hundred students, but more than three hundred turned up.

Out of that meeting grew an organization that soon would become one of the most courageous leaders of the civil rights movement, the Student Nonviolent Coordinating Committee. SNCC (its name was pronounced "snick") was committed to nonviolence and to using demonstrations to seek an end to segregation. SNCC called its guiding purpose "nonviolent direct action." SNCC's founders also demanded that they remain independent of other organizations, including that of Dr. King, who had hoped the students would become junior members of SCLC. The coordinating committee quickly developed a style that emphasized consensus, or making certain that virtually everyone agreed with a plan of action before it was adopted. Just taking a vote wasn't enough; everyone who was out in the thick of the battle, risking his or her life, had to agree. (These people called themselves field secretaries.) Sometimes SNCC's meetings went on for *days*, and people who observed the group would joke that SNCC was the most disorganized organization they had ever seen. But they acknowledged that SNCC's way of doing things seemed to work. A new organization, a new form of action, had joined the growing Movement.

Nonviolent direct action brought a new burst of excitement and imagination to the Movement. The form of protest that was used in Greensboro was extended far beyond the lunch counter. In Biloxi, a small city on Mississippi's Gulf of Mexico coast, some blacks conducted a "wade-in" at the beach. Whites fought back with violence, and ten Negroes were wounded by gunfire. In numerous other places, young people held sit-ins at public libraries, court-rooms, skating rinks, and other institutions of the segregated society.

James Lawson suggested to SNCC workers that when they were arrested in demonstrations, they should refuse to post bail. In that way, they could dramatize the injustice of the system. In most arrests, the person who is arrested can deposit some money (called bail, or bond money) with the court and be released "on bail" until it is time to appear in court for trial. The rule is that if the arrested person doesn't return for the trial, the court keeps the money. In serious crimes, such as murder or bank robbery, the court will take the bail money *and* send officers out to track down the defendant. As sit-in demonstrations filled the South's jails, many who ran the system were happy to accept bail money of twenty-five or fifty dollars and let the demonstrator go. There was an unspoken understanding that the student would not return for trial, that the city would be spared the expense of a trial (and the possibly negative publicity), and that the court would make a little money and forget about the whole thing. When demonstrators adopted a jail,-no-bail attitude and refused to post bond, the system was often thrown into confusion—which was exactly what the demonstrators wanted.

The Freedom Ride, another form of activism, was brought to the Movement by the Congress of Racial Equality. As was the case with the Montgomery bus boycott and the Greensboro sit-ins, the Freedom Ride was not a brand-new form of protest. It, too, was built on what had gone before. In this case, opponents of segregation had climbed aboard interstate buses in 1947 and ridden through the South. They defied the rules of the states and the bus companies that seating on the buses must be segregated (despite a 1946 Supreme Court decision that such seating was unconstitutional). They were arrested and imprisoned.

In the spring of 1961, CORE organized a new Freedom Ride through the South. By now not only the Supreme Court, but also the agency of the federal government that regulated interstate buses, the Interstate Commerce Commission, had ruled segregation in such transportation to be illegal. Thirteen people, ranging in age from eighteen to sixty-one, headed south on buses from Washington, D.C., on May 4. Seven of them were black, six were white. (Some left during the ride, and others joined it.) Their plan was to reach New Orleans on May 17, the seventh anniversary of the *Brown* decision. They announced beforehand that they intended to remain nonviolent. They informed President John F. Kennedy of their plans, in hopes that the federal government would make sure that its laws and Constitution were being obeyed.

There were no major problems as the group traveled through Virginia, North Carolina, South Carolina, and Georgia. But when the group (now in two buses) crossed the state line into Alabama, major trouble started. A mob of whites met one of the buses in Anniston, Alabama, slashed its tires, and set it on fire. A single brave employee of the Alabama State Highway Patrol, a white man who had been travelling in civilian clothes on the bus, kept the mob from attacking the riders. Twelve passengers had to be taken to the hospital. In Birmingham, Alabama's largest city, riders were badly beaten by a rioting mob. The local police did nothing to stop the riot. They were under the control of an extreme segregationist, Eugene Connor, who was known by his friends and enemies as "Bull." (Later, it was learned that the Federal Bureau of Investigation knew of plans by the Ku Klux Klan, the terrorist group, to attack the riders, but the FBI did nothing about it. Throughout the Movement years, the FBI opposed those who wanted to bring an end to segregation.)

After the Birmingham riot, the bus drivers declined to go to the next stop, which was Montgomery. The Alabama governor, John Patterson, refused to protect the riders. The original CORE riders gave up the idea of the ride and flew to New Orleans.

But if the Alabama segregationists thought they had won the battle of segregated transportation, they were wrong. A new group of Freedom Riders formed. This time they included many of the demonstrators from the colleges in Nashville—the same young people who had helped to form the student protest movement a year before. One of those who had been on the original ride, a Nashville student named John Lewis, signed up for the second one as well. The leader of the second ride was a young woman, Diane Nash, a native of Chicago who went to Nashville to go to school and who had been outraged at the segregation she found there.

When the new riders arrived in Birmingham, they were arrested. In their case, as in the case of many of the arrests in the Movement years, the charges had no connection with any actual crimes. These arrests were called "protective custody," which meant the police were trying to make it appear that, instead of jailing the riders for exercising their constitutional rights, they were protecting them from harm. Bull Connor had his police officers take the students out of jail and drive them back to the Tennessee state line, where they were dumped out of the police cars. The students managed to get back to Birmingham within a few hours, and the ride continued.

When the Freedom Ride arrived in Montgomery, which is about a hundred miles south of Birmingham, it was met by a mob of about a thousand people. The city police, who were ordinarily supposed to keep order in such situations, were nowhere in sight. The mob beat the riders for two hours; when ambulances arrived to take the victims to a hospital, the mob forced their drivers to leave. Several persons, including an observer from the U.S. Justice Department, were beaten seriously. Finally, officers from the Alabama Highway Patrol arrived, and the riot ended. The patrol was headed by a professional policeman named Floyd Mann, who did not necessarily agree with the riders' aims but who believed it was his duty to uphold the law and prevent violence.

President John Kennedy and his brother, Attorney General Robert F. Kennedy, sent lawyers to federal court to prevent the local authorities from allowing further violence. They also sent four hundred U.S. marshals (the officers who maintain peace in the federal courts) and other federal officers to Montgomery. One of the marshals' first jobs was to prevent a screaming mob from invading a black church where Martin Luther King, Jr., who had flown to Alabama after the rides started, was leading a mass meeting.

The Power of Nonviolence

Throughout it all, Governor Patterson did little to prevent violence. He repeatedly demanded that the federal officials leave. Much of the time he was at odds with his highway patrol chief, Floyd Mann, who welcomed federal assistance and did his best to keep violence down.

As was often the case in the Southern movement, the efforts by segregationist officials such as Patterson to put down demonstrations only succeeded in making the freedom seekers more determined. As Diane Nash put it, "They beat us, and we're stronger than ever." All over the nation, from California to New York to Minneapolis, blacks and whites decided to go on their *own* Freedom Rides. They headed south on buses, stopping in Birmingham and Montgomery (where federal marshals kept the peace) and then riding to Jackson, Mississippi, where they were arrested when they stepped off their buses. (The charges included "refusing to obey an officer" when the officer told them they could not desegregate bus terminals that had been ordered desegregated by the U.S. Supreme Court. Through the Movement years, those who took part made it clear that, while they wanted to be law-abiding citizens, they could and would not cooperate with laws that were clearly wrong.)

Attorney General Robert Kennedy asked the demonstrators for a "cooling-off period," but the demonstrators declined. Then he suggested that they concentrate their efforts on registering voters, rather than taking part in direct action. Some of the young people *did* want to move into voter registration, because they believed that was where real challenges to the system could be made, but they also wanted to continue the transportation demonstrations.

Soon prominent people from the North—religious leaders, politicians—were riding buses and flying airplanes to the South to show their sympathy for the jailed Freedom Riders. On June 1, not quite a month after the original ride had started, a reporter wrote that one of the bus terminals in Montgomery had been "quietly desegregated." Gradually, the other transportation services in the South followed suit.

Once it gained speed and momentum, the civil rights movement was a wide, huge movement that affected every corner of life in the South and, to a lesser extent, in the nation. Different communities reacted in different ways to the Supreme Court's school desegregation decision, to the Montgomery bus boycott, to the Greensboro sit-ins, and to the Freedom Rides. Some communities quietly dropped their racial barriers and never made the newspapers. In many other places, particularly the smaller towns and rural areas of the Deep South, it might seem that nothing had changed. The "white" and "colored" water fountains stayed in place, the children continued going to separate schools, and the buses (if there were any) remained segregated.

But it was impossible to estimate the effect that the big events of the Movement had on the minds and hearts of individual Negroes—and whites, too, for that matter— even in places where nothing seemed to happen. Television was becoming the medium by which more and more people got their information about what was happening in the rest of the world; segregation might still be firmly in place in Jones's Crossroads, Georgia, or Davisville, Alabama, but the citizens of those places could turn on the TV and see what was going on elsewhere, and they knew that a huge Movement was in the making.

It would be wrong to think that the Movement was just a series of big, exciting events, conveniently named after cities—Greensboro, Montgomery, Birmingham—but it is true that those were the mileposts by which the struggle proceeded. The *Brown* decision established the federal government's position on discrimination in education. Greensboro put the nation on notice that young black people were not going to accept the status of second-class citizens when they went downtown. Montgomery and the Freedom Rides forced the nation to face up to discrimination in public transportation. One by one, the walls were coming down. In some places, they were coming down fairly easily. In others, it took mighty doses of energy, talent, brain power—and, above all, courage—to even start to put a crack in them.

Everybody knew that the thickest, strongest walls were in Mississippi, Alabama, the southern parts of Georgia, and parts of Virginia. Most of those were the areas where, in slavery days, the plantation system had thrived. Those were the places where the black population was greatest and where the white citizens feared what would happen if Negroes suddenly got power. If black people could vote, they might kick out of office the sheriff who had treated them so cruelly and who had allowed a white lynch mob to snatch a black man from his jail cell. They might remove the county commissioner or the legislator who had campaigned for so long on promises of "segregation forever," and they might trade in the racist school board for one that was dedicated to real equality. They might eliminate the economic injustice that was such an important part of the system and that dictated that black people would earn far less than whites who did the same work, or that farm workers could be thrown off their land for not showing proper respect to a white person.

It was fears of these kinds that made it so difficult for blacks to achieve progress in Albany, a small city in southern Georgia's plantation district. What also made it difficult was the way Albany's white leaders refused even to consider requests for change during the summer of 1962. Instead of allowing white mobs to inflict violence on Negro protestors and their sympathizers, Albany simply arrested everybody who protested (using laws that were clearly in violation of the Constitution and Supreme Court rulings) and put them in jail.

The members of the Albany Movement, as the civil rights protest was known, asked federal officials in Washington to help them, but no help came. It seemed that John and Robert Kennedy didn't know how to deal with a situation in which the segregationists didn't use violence. They could have brought lawsuits in federal courts to force Albany to obey the nation's law, but they didn't. Instead, they praised the Albany officials for preventing violence. Once, they even prosecuted in federal court some of those who had done the protesting.

One result of all this—of white Albany's actions and the federal government's inactions—was a damaging blow to the Movement's morale. Albany, some observers said, was a defeat for the Movement. But others argued that it was an important step in the growth of the Movement. It gave freedom fighters experience in dealing with another face of the complicated system of segregation.

The Power of Nonviolence

*   *   *

In the minds of many who were starting to think of themselves as full-time Movement workers, Mississippi was the toughest place of all. If there was any doubt about that opinion, it disappeared in the fall of 1962, when a native Mississippian who was black, James Meredith, tried to enter the University of Mississippi.

Meredith had followed the rules. As a high school student his essay "Why I Am Proud to Be an American" had won an American Legion essay contest. He served his country in the air force for nine years. Then he returned home to Mississippi, determined to get a good education.

He applied by mail to the University of Mississippi at Oxford, the school that is known as Ole Miss. This was (and is) the school that produced many of those who run the state—its politicians, business leaders, lawyers, and teachers. Ole Miss had no black students. The school replied to Meredith with a cordial letter: "We are very pleased to know of your interest in becoming a member of our student body." When the school's officials found out Meredith was black, however, they changed their minds. They told Meredith he could not enter. Meredith and Movement lawyers brought a lawsuit, and finally the federal courts ordered the school to admit him. Even that wasn't easy. One of the federal judges ruled at one point that it was impossible for Meredith to be denied admission because of his race. The reason, he said, was that the university was "not a racially segregated institution." Higher courts easily saw through this ridiculous thinking.

Meredith finally did enter Old Miss, on the night of September 30, 1962, in the middle of a riot that left two people, one of them a news reporter, dead. White students

49

at the university were part of the mob, along with hundreds of outsiders from Mississippi and other Southern states. Once again, U.S. marshals and other federal officials had to preserve the peace. They had help from the U.S. Army and a large group of National Guard troopers, who were called into uniform by orders of President John Kennedy. Around two hundred people were injured. Most of them were federal officials. The state, led by Governor Ross Barnett, not only did little to prevent the violence, but actively encouraged it. When he was campaigning for office, Barnett and his supporters wore buttons that said, "Never, Never"—referring to his promise to never let desegregation happen in Mississippi.

After his admission, Ole Miss students made life horrible for Meredith everywhere he went. But the young man, accompanied by soldiers and marshals, went to class and earned his degree. On the day he graduated, beneath his cap and gown, Meredith wore the same clothes he had worn on the day he entered. He also wore one of Ross Barnett's "Never, Never" buttons. But he wore it upside down.

James Meredith's awful experience at Ole Miss won the sympathy of many Americans who were able to witness the way the system treated a Negro who wanted to play by the country's rules, who tried to better himself through getting the best possible education. Those people who rioted on the night of Meredith's entry to the University of Mississippi, and who harassed him for months afterward, did far more harm to their cause of segregation than they imagined. A few months after the Old Miss riot, when a federal court ordered Clemson University in South

Carolina to obey a federal court order to desegregate, things went smoothly. The reason, said the people who ran South Carolina, was that they didn't want "another Old Miss."

An even bigger example of the segregationists' tendency to hurt their own cause came in the spring of 1963, when the Southern Christian Leadership Conference began demonstrations in Birmingham, Alabama.

Birmingham had been the scene of much violence against black people. It was not unusual for bombs to go off in the middle of the night, destroying the homes of outspoken black leaders such as the Reverend Fred Shuttlesworth, who had no patience with segregation and didn't mind saying so. At the official level, Birmingham was a strictly segregationist city. The public safety commissioner, Bull Connor, was known around the world. The mayor, Arthur Hanes, was almost as dedicated to segregation. When a federal court ordered Birmingham to open its parks and other places to people of all colors, these leaders closed them instead.

Things got so bad that Birmingham's progressive voters (who were mostly white, since blacks had difficulty registering there) removed Hanes and Connor from office and changed the city's form of government. Then Hanes and Connor refused to leave.

In the midst of all this turmoil, SCLC began demonstrations. Martin Luther King, Jr., and his colleagues in SCLC, who had shared in the defeat in Albany the previous summer, chose Birmingham for a very simple reason: Birmingham was as bad as any place in the South, and if Birmingham could be made to change, *anyplace* in the South could be made to change. They also thought it was quite likely that the segregationists in Birmingham would use violence, as they had before, and that this would win the sympathy of Americans of good will. The Movement's planners made it clear that they did not *want* violence. The whites were always free to *not* use guns and clubs and bombs. But if they did use them, the Movement would benefit.

The segregationists did use violence. When blacks tried to march downtown to conduct protests or when they visited white churches to hold "kneel-ins," Bull Connor and his policemen directed high-pressure fire hoses at them and turned vicious police dogs on them. Many of the victims of this official violence, which went on for five weeks, were children. News photographers took pictures of them being assaulted by the fire hoses or bitten by the dogs, and the pictures were flashed around the world. Suddenly America became very ashamed of Birmingham. President John Kennedy explained rather weakly that he could do nothing about the situation because no federal laws were being violated.

The Supreme Court, in the meantime, ruled that Bull Connor and Arthur Hanes had to leave their jobs, and the new government took power. The Court also found that Birmingham's segregation laws—the ones requiring separate water fountains, segregated buses, and even separation in churches on Sunday morning—were unconstitutional. The violence receded in Birmingham.

After Birmingham, demonstrations grew rapidly throughout the South. Martin Luther King, Jr., had been right: Birmingham was the key. The months of shameful violence prodded President Kennedy to ask Congress to pass a new civil rights bill, a collection of new laws protecting minority rights and promising remedies to segregation that were stronger than any previous ones in the nation's history.

Birmingham may have been the key, but it was not the end. There was much more for the Movement to accomplish.

FIVE

Freedom Summers

I t might seem that once one of the Movement's major battles was finished, that issue could be considered settled. If a lunch counter desegregated, then that would be an end to lunch counter discrimination. That was certainly not the way things happened in the sixties, and it's not the way things happen anytime in the real world.

Although James Meredith finally was able to enter the University of Mississippi at Oxford, that did not mean that black people were suddenly free to attend formerly all-white schools in that state, or in several others. Nor did it mean that when they did attend, they would be welcomed by their fellow students and teachers. Blacks who followed Meredith to Ole Miss found many obstacles in their way—but not nearly as many as had faced that courageous young man.

Change was slow in coming, too, to Birmingham. The voters there changed the city's form of government to remove the bitter segregationists from office, but that did not mean all was sweetness and light in Alabama's largest city. Bombs still went off from time to time, and the authorities did little to bring to justice those who were exploding them.

The sit-ins that took place at Greensboro and at dozens of Southern cities afterward did not automatically mean that black people were welcome in all the places where their money was welcome. *Public accommodations*, the term used to apply to places that supposedly served the public, such as stores, waiting rooms at bus, train, and airplane terminals, and public libraries, were open to everyone in some places, but they remained stubbornly segregated in others. As usual, Mississippi and Alabama proved to be the most resistant places about accepting change.

In almost all parts of the South, local and state officials dragged their heels on school desegregation. They would think up new schemes to keep the old segregated system in place, and the federal courts would knock those schemes down, and the officials would try to think up more. In the meantime, a lot of time passed. Black and white children who in a few years would be expected to become the adult leaders of the South continued to grow up in school systems where they stood no chance of getting to know one another.

It was clear to anyone who looked closely that in the South, more than anywhere else in the United States, progress would depend on everyone's working together. The South has always been the poorest region in the nation, and its inhabitants have always been among the worst educated. The expense of operating two separate systems, one for whites and one for blacks (and in some places, another one for Indians!), only made the region more impoverished. It was obvious that eliminating racial barriers could help more than any other single thing to lift the South out of its poverty. But the South's politicians seemed afraid to take that step. They feared that if they did, they would be thrown out of office by segregationist whites.

That fear would not have arisen, of course, if black people had been allowed to vote. If they had, they could have helped elect people who wanted to serve the whole community, not just a part of it; people who put their region's progress ahead of personal considerations. Already, in the summer of 1963, efforts were being made to bring that vote to people to whom it had been denied. Organizations such as the National Association for the Advancement of Colored People had long promoted voter registration campaigns. Their local officials had been threatened and intimidated, but they continued anyway. Younger activists from the Student Nonviolent Coordinating Committee and the Congress of Racial Equality, calling themselves organizers, started moving into small towns in the South and talking with people about the need for voting. The first thing they had to explain was why voting was so important—why it was worth the trouble that might come from the segregationists if a black man or woman went down to register at the county courthouse. It was almost always a courthouse where only a handful of Negroes had been allowed to register before and where the officials would ask complicated questions and give tough tests that they never gave to white applicants.

There was much change still to be accomplished.

The riot at Ole Miss proved to some Southern governors that the days of defiance over desegregation in colleges and universities were over. But George Wallace, who succeeded John Patterson as the governor of Alabama, insisted on showing the white voters that he could still defy the courts. When federal courts ordered the University of Alabama to admit two Negroes as students, Wallace said he would "stand in the schoolhouse door" to keep them from entering. Actually, Wallace planned to allow the students in; he just wanted to do some playacting to fool his segregationist constituents. When federal officials arrived with the students, Wallace stepped aside (he was standing in an actual doorway on the university's campus at Tuscaloosa, Alabama) and they entered.

On June 12, 1963, the day after the students entered the University of Alabama, the Movement lost one of its real heroes. Medgar E. Evers, the NAACP leader in Mississippi, was murdered by a hidden gunman as he was entering his home in Jackson. Once again, violence against the Movement and its leaders served only to bring more people into the struggle and to make those who were already there more determined to defeat segregation and racism. They were in the battle until the end, even if it meant they would have to give their lives for the Movement, as Medgar Evers had done.

By the summer of 1963, also, a lot of people were no longer thinking of the Movement as simply a Southern struggle. Black people in the North, the Midwest, and the West were looking around themselves and seeing that there might be laws on the books outlawing discrimination in employment, but *they* were exploited economically, too, just like black people in the South. Their laws in New York and Chicago and Los Angeles said there would be no housing segregation, but *they* lived in all-black neighborhoods, too, and they were likely to get the runaround if they went house- or apartment-hunting in white neighborhoods. They had no trouble registering to vote and casting their ballots on election day, but the sort of elected leadership they got was not as responsive to their needs as it should have been. The summer of 1963 marked a great rise in the recognition by blacks outside the South (many of whom had fled the South years before because of segregation) that discrimination could be found everywhere in America.

The impatience of the Northerners was increased when they read about the gains that were being made, often at great personal cost, by antisegregationists in the South. "If they can put their lives and jobs on the line for something we all believe in," the thinking went, "maybe *we* should, too." And there was another factor that helped turn 1963 into the year that the struggle became an all-American cause. When John F. Kennedy was elected to the presidency in 1960, he brought a great deal of hope to American people who were downtrodden or who sympathized with the downtrodden. Kennedy was a member of a wealthy Massachusetts family and had no personal experience with being poor or exploited. (He did know something about being discriminated against, though. He was a Catholic, and in his campaign for the presidency many voters had expressed reservations about electing America's first Catholic chief executive.) But Kennedy held out a vision of a new America, one that would move past hatred and racism into the space age. As he dealt with Movement confrontations at Birmingham and Ole Miss, it was clear that he was a believer in racial equality. (He was also a politician, however, and his critics say he leaned over backward to avoid angering Southern governors. Kennedy also appointed some federal judges in the South who were strong segregationists.)

One outgrowth of the widening struggle to end segregation in South and North was the March on Washington.

It was organized by A. Philip Randolph, the black labor leader who had successfully threatened President Franklin D. Roosevelt with a similar march back in 1941. The issue back then was equality in employment, and the same issue prompted Randolph and his assistant, Bayard Rustin, to plan another march in the summer of 1963. The official name of the demonstration was to be "March on Washington for Jobs." Only after Randolph and Rustin realized that freedom-lovers everywhere wanted to participate did they enlarge the name to "March on Washington for Jobs and Freedom."

The planners thought that at most 100,000 people might turn up for the march, which would take place on the grounds of the Capitol. Many of them would be union members from big cities in the North. They would ride chartered buses to the event.

At first, the Kennedy administration opposed the march. It, and many newspaper editorial writers, expressed fears that violence might break out. When it became apparent that the march was going to take place whether or not the Kennedys approved of it, the president and his brother tried to make it *their* march. It could be, they figured, a demonstration in favor of a new civil rights bill that the Kennedys wanted to pass. Randolph and Rustin were used to dealing with politicians, however, and they kept tight control of the march.

When the march took place, it was the largest demonstration in the history of America. Not 100,000, but

200,000, people turned up. And they didn't all come down on their day off from the big cities of the North; they arrived by the thousands in cars and chartered buses and on trains from the deepest and most segregated places of the South—from Mississippi, and Alabama, and Albany, Georgia; from Danville, Virginia, where in the spring the police had beaten demonstrators every bit as savagely as Bull Connor's men had in Birmingham.

There was no violence. The March on Washington was perhaps the friendliest, most loving gathering that ever took place on the Capitol Mall. (There was, however, some offstage argument among some of the organizers about how critical the speakers should be of the federal government.) And the march will always be remembered as the place where Martin Luther King, Jr., delivered his famous I-have-a-dream speech. That speech ended with the words from the spiritual, "Free at last! Free at last! Thank God A-mighty, we are free at last!"

After the March, much of the nation looked on Dr. King as *the* leader of the civil rights movement. That was unfair to the many others who provided leadership for the Movement, and it incorrectly gave the impression that the struggle consisted of one leader and thousands of followers. In actuality, much of the Movement was "leaders" scrambling to keep up with the long and rapid strides of their "followers."

The wonderful day in Washington ended, and marchers returned to their homes in the North, Midwest, West, and South. For many of the young heroes of the Movement, the March was a day-long vacation from the hard work of organizing, demonstrating, and registering voters. By now, the civil rights organizations that were most active on the ground level, SNCC and CORE, were operating projects in small and large towns and rural areas all over the South. Most of them were efforts to register voters, but in some places, segregation and discrimination were so bad that the organizers' first task was to try to tear away the layer of fear that covered the black community. They did this by leading demonstrations and by doing things that they knew would result in their own arrests. Only after the fear was gone could people find the courage to go down to the courthouse to register.

Slowly but surely, the segregationists were losing one of their most important weapons. No longer were black people in the South afraid of going to the white man's jail. In fact, some Movement people began talking about jail as a "badge of courage"—as proof of involvement in the struggle.

Once again, a moment of triumph for the Movement was followed by a time of sadness. Eighteen days after the March on Washington was held, a bomb exploded on a Sunday morning at the Sixteenth Street Baptist Church, in Birmingham, Alabama, one of the churches used by the Movement for its mass meetings. Four girls who were attending Sunday school were killed. Two were fourteen years old, one was eleven, and one was ten.

The nation was outraged at this most recent cowardly attack. President Kennedy and his brother worked harder on preparing the civil rights legislation they had started after the spring 1963 violence in Birmingham. The State of Alabama, which in the past had rarely even tried to punish those responsible for mob violence, arrested three men. The charge was not murder but illegal possession of dynamite. They were tried and convicted—also unusual for Alabama. But they were sentenced to six months in jail and fines of $100.

A few weeks after the Birmingham bombing, in November 1963, President John Kennedy was assassinated in Dallas, Texas. The nation was thrown into turmoil and doubt. What sort of president would Vice President Lyndon B. Johnson make? Would he care at all about the dreams that Kennedy had promised? Johnson was a Southern white man; would the Movement have an even harder time getting the cooperation of the federal government?

The nation and the Movement received their answer quickly. Johnson soon got Congress to pass a massive law, a "war on poverty." Its backers argued that poverty, and not just senseless racism, was at the bottom of much discrimination in America. The program promised to improve conditions for poor people throughout the country, not just in the South.

At the same time, the civil rights bill that the Kennedys had drawn up after the Birmingham violence and church bombing was making its way through Congress. President Johnson was a strong backer, although some of his advisers worried that if he supported it, he might hurt his chances of being elected. The presidential term of the assassinated John Kennedy would expire at the end of 1964, and Johnson was running for the job. His Republican opponent, Senator Barry Goldwater, was a conservative who had little good to say about integration, desegregation, or the Movement. The senator had what he called a Southern strategy, by which he went after the votes of Southern whites who were upset over what they saw as Johnson's too-close friendship with black people. Johnson backed the legislation anyway, and when Congress passed the Civil Rights Act of 1964 in the summer of that year, Johnson proudly signed it into law. Johnson won the Democratic party's nomination, and in the fall he was elected president for a full term. He went on to become one of America's strongest presidents on civil rights issues.

The Movement, or rather its younger members, had their own Southern strategy in 1963. They had known for some time that the key to true change in the United States was the ballot box. All the desegregated lunch counters and bus terminals in the world wouldn't make much difference if the black Southerner could not go to the voting place on election day and help elect his or her president, senator, congressional representative, governor, state or local judges, county commissioner, and mayor. They knew, too, that black people in the South *would* vote if they were just given the opportunity. In the fall of 1963, representatives of SNCC, CORE, and interested groups of college students from the North held a mock election in Mississippi. They wanted to prove to anybody who was watching—and they hoped the Kennedys were watching— that if black people had the right to vote without being penalized, they would use that right. An estimated 90,000 people took part in the "election." The event was not a real election, but it clearly made its organizers' point.

Over the winter of 1963–1964, representatives from SNCC, CORE, and the NAACP made plans for what they called Freedom Summer. It would take place in the summer of 1964, and its main aim was to help black people enter the American political process. The campaign would be held in Mississippi, where SNCC and CORE would do much of the work, and in Louisiana, where CORE had a long history of organizing.

There would be trips down to the courthouse to register voters, but there also would be "freedom schools," where people could learn about citizenship—about the process they would be entering when they did exercise their right to vote. Later in the summer, the organizers hoped, delegates from a new political party would go from Mississippi to the Democratic National Convention, where President Johnson was seeking his party's nomination. The new party, called the Mississippi Freedom Democratic party, would argue that the *regular* delegates to the convention from Mississippi—the people who would cast the votes to select the party's nominee for president—did not represent all of Mississippi. They were all white, and they represented a political party that discriminated against Negroes. By contrast, the Mississippi Freedom Democratic party, or MFDP, was open to anyone, regardless of skin color.

Freedom Summer 1964 had another important characteristic. Its organizers would seek out and invite volunteers, many of them white college students, from the North.

One of the saddest lessons that the heroes of the Movement had learned in the years since they started risking their lives was that the sympathy of the people who ran the nation was limited. Influential people from the North—newspaper editorial writers, elected politicians in Washington—*talked* about their belief in equality and ending discrimination, but they didn't *do* very much about it if only black lives were involved. It was as if even the people who considered themselves liberals and opponents of segregation thought a black life was somehow worth less than a white one.

The organizers knew that that situation would change if white people—especially white *young* people, the sons and daughters of prominent business and political leaders—had *their* lives on the line, too. So they invited these white young people to take part in Freedom Summer. Much of their recruiting was done on the campuses of America's most prestigious universities in the North.

The plan worked. When the young Northern whites arrived in the South and started their work in the dangerous towns and crossroads and dirt roads and plantations of Mississippi and Louisiana, a lot of older Northern whites paid very close attention to what was going on and to the dangers that were involved. There was a good reason for this: They were the young people's parents. From a thousand to seventeen hundred of the volunteers went to the Deep South. They had been told that they would not take charge of the organizing effort but rather would assist the organizers and local people. Students who were going to school to learn to be teachers and historians and political scientists served as instructors in the Freedom Schools; medical students helped out in the community centers. Even a group of volunteer lawyers went south to help in legal actions.

Soon after the summer project began, there was a tragic proof of the planners' theory that the nation would pay more attention if white lives were threatened. Three young people disappeared one June night in Neshoba County, Mississippi. One of them, James Chaney, twenty-one, a CORE worker from Mississippi, was black. The other two were white: Michael Schwerner, twenty-four, a social worker from New York City who had worked several months for CORE in Mississippi; and Andrew Goodman, twenty-one, a student from New York who had responded to the call for summer volunteers.

At first, the Federal Bureau of Investigation paid little attention to the case—as was its habit in most situations involving civil rights. But there was a difference this time. White people were involved. President Johnson sent J. Edgar Hoover, the FBI head who previously had expressed little but scorn for Movement leaders, to Mississippi to coordinate the investigation. Hundreds of FBI agents followed, and before long the agents found someone who was willing to tell them, in exchange for $30,000, where the young men's bodies could be found and the names of those who had murdered them.

The three had been killed by members of the Ku Klux Klan, acting in cooperation with the local police authorities. Eventually seven men, including a Neshoba County deputy sheriff, went to prison for the crime. It was the first time that the federal government had actually acted in a case of this sort. Civil rights activists were glad to see the change, but they were saddened by their knowledge that it would have been a different story indeed if all three of the murdered young men had been black.

Not long afterward, President Johnson signed into law the Civil Rights Act of 1964. It was the most comprehensive package of such information to date. Perhaps its most important feature was insuring that blacks had the right to vote in federal elections. But the act did nothing to stop a series of summertime riots by black residents of the Harlem community of New York City and a number of other Northern cities. Experts who studied the riots said that the Northerners were demonstrating their anger and frustration at the conditions of their own neighborhoods, which they began to call black ghettoes. (*Ghetto* is the term for a part of a city where a racial or ethnic group is forced to live. Originally the term referred to Jews, who were restricted to certain sections in European towns.)

In August 1964, the Democrats went to Atlantic City, New Jersey, to hold their presidential nominating convention. When the Mississippi Freedom Democratic party showed up, the leadership of the national Democratic party rejected its claim that it was the only group that properly could represent all the Democrats in the state. President Johnson and his backers, who were afraid of losing support from Southern white members of the party, proposed a compromise plan that would give the Freedom party only token representation at the convention. The Freedom party angrily refused the offer.

The rejection was a severe blow to the Movement organizers, who had both devoted and risked their lives—and seen some of their number *give* their lives—in an attempt to win one of America's most basic rights and one that most Americans took for granted: the right to vote. They left Atlantic City and returned to the dangerous towns, cities, and rural areas of the Deep South. They were disappointed, confused, dejected, and exhausted.

By one way of figuring it, Freedom Summer had been a great success. Black people who lived in the most oppressive parts of the South—the places where fear and terror had been the greatest—had begun to overcome their fear. And everybody had learned that overcoming fear was the first step in creating real change. But there were sad statistics, too: When Freedom Summer ended, six people had been murdered. There had been thirty-five shooting incidents in which three people were injured. Thirty buildings had been bombed. Thirty-five churches had been burned down. At least eighty people had been beaten.

Some of the heroes of the Movement were talking about giving up on nonviolence. They might be able to accomplish more, they thought, if they could fight back when attacked. Some were ready to give up, as well, on the idea of America; they spoke of moving away, going to Africa. But most of them kept plugging away, kept the Movement moving.

Some left Mississippi and went to a place in southernmost Alabama, where conditions were every bit as bad as Mississippi. The place was Selma, a small city fifty miles from Montgomery, where blacks had been treated like dirt. Jim Clark, the sheriff of Dallas County (of which Selma was the county seat), ruled the place with an iron hand. He was a strong, violent foe of desegregation.

In 1963, when Dallas County blacks went to the courthouse to register to vote, they were turned away. Representatives of the FBI and the Justice Department who were on hand just stood there; they did nothing to help the citizens secure their rights. Sheriff Clark and some of his followers chased the Negroes away from the county office, and when the blacks ran up the steps of the federal building, Clark came after them. It looked as if the government in Washington was unwilling to defend even its own territory against racism in Dallas County. To some of the veterans of the Freedom Summer in Mississippi and the disappointment of Atlantic City, Selma looked like a new challenge. It would surely provide valuable confrontation.

SIX

Selma and Beyond

Selma was chosen by youthful organizers from both the Student Nonviolent Coordinating Committee and the Southern Christian Leadership Conference because it was such a tough place. The black people in Selma and surrounding counties were scared of what might happen to them if they tried to vote or exercise other rights. If change could be brought to Selma, the activists reasoned, it could come anyplace.

There were indications as early as September 1963 that white people in Selma were uneasy about what might happen, too. After the first activists arrived in the town, the white leaders ran a full-page advertisement in the local newspaper saying that blacks and whites had lived peacefully together in Selma for many years and that they would do so again after the activists left. Some black people thought this was a way of saying to them, "You may have some protection while these outsiders are in town, but when they go away, it'll just be you and us."

"Us," in Selma, included Sheriff Jim Clark and his

posse, a group of deputies who rode around on horseback. The sheriff and his men had terrible reputations in the black community, but they were just what the Movement organizers wanted. By now, the Movement's strategy planners knew that violence from the white side, even though it was an awful thing, could only help the Movement more. It would bring sympathy from the rest of the nation, and it would put pressure on politicians to enforce existing laws and pass new ones that would insure black Americans the same rights and freedoms as anybody else. Such violence almost always occurred against people who were totally peaceful. They were walking down a city street, or seeking to enter a public building, or carrying protest signs, or otherwise exercising their freedom of speech—actions that are protected for all Americans by the United States Constitution.

Some people wondered back then, and it still might be wondered today, if it was right to move deliberately into a situation where it was almost certain that violence would result. The answer is that the segregationists always had the opportunity to react *without* violence. The choice was theirs. They could have agreed to follow the law and the Constitution and to avoid violence. And, of course, the federal government could have stepped in and prevented any violence, but it hardly ever did unless one of its own court orders was being violated.

When Martin Luther King, Jr., went to Selma in early 1965, it was to lead marches to the voter registration office at the Dallas County courthouse. Dr. King hoped the demonstrations (and the reaction they might cause from Sheriff Clark and other segregationists) would prod Lyndon Johnson and other federal officials to do more to guarantee the vote for Negroes. One way this could be done, thought Dr. King, was by bringing in federal registrars to do the work of county officials in registering voters.

The protests in Selma caught the interest of blacks (not to mention whites) in counties and communities surrounding Dallas County. The area was poor, and in many ways it still resembled the cotton-growing region that it had been during plantation days. When blacks started similar demonstrations in the little town of Marion, to the west of Selma, members of the Alabama Highway Patrol, who now were under the control of a strict segregationist, moved in and attacked them with clubs. One young man, Jimmy Lee Jackson, was shot to death by a policeman.

By March 1965, Selma was ready. Dr. King and other civil rights leaders planned a march from Selma to the state capitol in Montgomery, fifty miles to the east, over a highway that was named after the President of the Confederacy, Jefferson Davis. On March 7, a Sunday, more than five hundred blacks and whites started the march. They got only as far as the Edmund Pettus Bridge, which takes the highway across the Alabama River, on Selma's eastern side. There the state police and Sheriff Clark's posse were waiting. Some were on horseback. Some carried clubs and some carried whips. The police and Sheriff Clark's men beat the marchers bloody.

Within minutes, the world was looking at photographs of what would be known as Selma's Bloody Sunday. As with the fire hoses and police dogs and the bombed-out church in Birmingham, as with the murdered civil rights workers in Mississippi, the violence from the segregationists only made the Movement stronger.

Bloody Sunday also brought the Movement's friends to

Selma by car, bus, and planeload. People from around the nation, including those who had never taken part in a demonstration before, were so enraged at what had happened that they hurried to Selma, determined to finish the march. They went to mass meetings and sang the Movement's anthem, "We Shall Overcome," and they visited white churches to remind Alabamans that discrimination was not a Christian thing to do. One clergyman who came from Boston, James Reeb, was among a group that was beaten by a white mob. He died from his wounds. President Johnson telephoned the man's wife to tell her how sorry he was. Movement people sadly noted that the president had not called Jimmy Lee Jackson's family after *his* death. Reeb was white, and Jackson was black.

A new march was scheduled for March 21, two weeks after Bloody Sunday. Thousands of people streamed into town. Dozens of reporters arrived from newspapers and television stations. Governor George Wallace had refused to provide any state protection for the marchers, and President Johnson announced that he was placing the Alabama National Guard, which normally is under the rule of the governor, under federal control. Wallace and Johnson met. Apparently it was not a productive meeting, for afterward the president announced: "I have made clear, whether the governor agrees or not, that law and order will prevail in Alabama, that the people's rights to peacefully assemble will be preserved, and that their constitutional rights will be protected."

Two days after the meeting, and less than a week before the march was scheduled to take place, President Johnson announced that he would ask Congress to pass the strongest voting rights legislation in the nation's history. The president spoke to a joint session of Congress, and his remarks were televised to the whole nation. He surprised many Americans when he said, of the Movement: "Their cause must be our cause, too. Because it's not just Negroes, but really it's all of us, who must overcome the crippling legacy of bigotry and injustice. And we *shall* overcome." When he uttered the most powerful words of the Movement's most moving anthem, Johnson came closer than any other president to proclaiming that the civil rights movement was *his* movement, too.

Two days later, the president's legislation went to Congress. And on March 21, the march took place. A federal judge decided that only three hundred people could take part in most of the march between Selma and Montgomery, but when the group got to the capitol on March 25, there were more than twenty-five thousand people on hand.

It was a moment of great joy, even greater than the one that August day in 1963 after the March on Washington. But, as always, there was also tragedy. A white woman who had come from Michigan to help with the march, Viola Gregg Liuzzo, was murdered by klansmen on the highway as she shuttled marchers between Selma and Montgomery. She was the mother of five children. One day later, President Johnson announced the arrest of four men in the shooting. An Alabama court refused to punish them at all on murder charges, but three of the men were found guilty of civil rights offenses in federal court. The fourth man, who testified against the others, was the same man who had been in the pay of the Federal Bureau of Investigation at the time of the violence against the Freedom Riders. He had participated in that attack, and yet the FBI continued to employ him. (Murder is not a federal offense in the United States. The individual states handle murder charges. But it *is* a federal offense to deprive people of their civil rights, and some of the killings of the civil rights era were prosecuted under this law.)

On August 6, Congress passed the Voting Rights Act of 1965. There was very little debate; the actions of Sheriff Clark, Governor Wallace, and others in Selma and the rest of Alabama had made it easy for members of Congress to vote for the bill. One of the law's provisions outlawed the tests that registrars had long used to discriminate against blacks who wanted to register. The most important part of the law provided, as Martin Luther King, Jr., had hoped, for federal registrars in Southern counties where discrimination had taken place in the past. *They* would register new voters from now on, not the local registrars who were such a prominent part of the segregated system.

When the Voting Rights Act was passed, the system of segregation started dying in the South. Political leaders who had shouted "segregation forever" (and translated it into "I'll get reelected forever") suddenly found enormous and frightening change looming on their horizons: They saw visions of black voters, coming for the first time into the polling places to decide whether *they*, the politicians, should remain in office or whether they should be replaced by someone more friendly to people of color. Many segregationist members of Congress, when they were voting on the new law, transformed themselves overnight into integrationists when they saw the law was certain to pass. It didn't take Southern governors, county commissioners, and mayors long to make the change, either.

As soon as the bill was enacted, federal registrars set up shop in fourteen counties in Alabama, Mississippi, and Louisiana—the places where discrimination was worst. Within a few months, voter registration in Mississippi went from an estimated 22,000 to 150,000. Less than five months after the bill was passed, federal officials were registering new voters in thirty-seven counties. Twenty months after passage, some 430,000 blacks had registered to vote throughout the South.

The change was quickly reflected in election returns. In the same month that the act was passed, a young SNCC staff worker from Atlanta, Julian Bond, was elected to the Georgia legislature. There had always been a coalition of black voters and progressive whites in the Georgia capital, and the coalition had assured the election of mayors and council members who were at least moderate in their racial views. But passage of the new act made the coalition even stronger. By 1966, barely a year after Bloody Sunday, a black sheriff was elected in Macon County, Alabama, which is the home of Tuskegee Institute, the school where Booker T. Washington had taught. In that same year, blacks gained a voting majority in Lowndes County, Alabama. Lowndes, through which the marchers had passed on their way to Montgomery, had been an even tougher place than Selma. When whites came up with a number of tricks to keep new black voters from running in the county's Democratic primary, the blacks formed their own party. On the ballot, the Democrats' symbol was a rooster; the Negroes named their group the Black Panther party and adopted the symbol of the black cat.

Whites—including those who had discriminated for decades against blacks at election time—immediately started complaining that the new party was some form of intimidation or discrimination and that the panther represented a violent animal that was threatening the minority (that is, the whites). (The situation became more confusing when a national organization, calling itself the Black Panther party, sprang up outside the South. The group was militant and not at all dedicated to nonviolence.)

But what really happened in Lowndes County and in other parts of the South where the Negro obtained the vote was that when black Americans got a chance to participate in the political process, they used their power wisely. In many counties in the Deep South, they could have done the reverse of what whites had been doing for a century. They could have voted all whites out of office and voted only blacks in. But they did not. They elected many black representatives, to be sure, but they also returned to office those whites who were not offensive to them and who they thought promised the best leadership for the country. They did, in fact, what good American citizens are supposed to do.

The Selma-to-Montgomery march and the dramatic changes in federal law that resulted from it marked the end of the beginning of the civil rights movement in America.

The victory at Selma meant that the Movement had achieved many of its major original goals. Education had been desegregated; public accommodations had been desegregated; the voting booth had been desegregated. That is not to say that all these areas were *integrated*. Although it was the nation's official policy that there should be no discrimination in public schools, for instance, there were plenty of schoolrooms that contained students of only one race. A reporter went back to Birmingham and found that the WHITE and COLORED signs were gone from the department store bathrooms but that customers had to ask for a key before they could use them. Was this a new attempt at segregation?

Discrimination in housing was about as bad after Selma as it had been before *Brown*. It was as hard to find any great improvement in employment. But the nation's policies had been changed. The initial barriers were down. And the biggest barrier of them all was gone, never to return: the fear, the terror that for so many years had kept so many black people in a form of slavery that was almost as bad as the one that had existed before.

No longer would an Alabama sheriff, or a Mississippi deputy, or a group of Ku Klux Klansmen, riding at night with their lights out and masks covering their faces, hold black people in the chains of terror. (They would try, however. In early 1966, some fifty crosses were burned across Mississippi—cross-burnings were part of the ritual of the Ku Klux Klan. And a few days later, Vernon Dahmer, a black grocer in Forrest County, Mississippi, who had provided support for the first voter registration workers to arrive in his state in 1960, was murdered.)

No longer could someone who wanted to be elected to public office, or who wanted to *continue* being elected, afford to ignore the needs and wishes of a large part of the electorate.

A victory had been won. But its very winning created a real crisis for some of those who had been the heroes of the Movement. What battles were they to fight now?

There were certainly plenty of battles still to be fought. Now that freedom existed on paper, there was the task of making it happen in reality. Now that people could vote, there remained the exhausting job of getting these newly active citizens interested in the political process and in voting. Now that there were laws on the books promising no discrimination in employment, there was the huge job of enforcing them. Movement people were fond of saying that the sit-ins at lunch counters were demonstrations for the right to buy a cup of coffee and a hamburger; now the much harder job was to win the economic justice that would allow blacks to *pay for* that food.

The young people of the Movement, the heroes, had grown up on danger. They had learned to set aside their fear of going to jail, or even of being hit on the head. They had tried hard to get used to the idea that their work in the Movement might even lead to their death.

Now, many people in the nation were saying the battles had been won. They were turning their attention in other directions. The war in Vietnam was occupying their thoughts more and more. This turning away was troubling to the young people of the Movement. They knew the struggle was a long way from being over, but they found that they had no real programs to deal with the new barriers that lay before them. A segregated lunch counter was one thing; how do you deal with economic inequality? It was a much tougher problem.

In both SNCC and CORE, the two organizations that had provided so many of the frontline soldiers in the battle, confusion and despair set in. SNCC's field secretaries started moving aimlessly from one project to another. Some of the activists started using drugs. Others grew interested in what was going on in Africa, where black nations were busily charting their futures after years of rule by outside whites. There were long and angry discussions in both SNCC and CORE about the value of nonviolence—the philosophy that only a few years before had been at the very heart of both organizations. By 1966, both groups were on record as being in favor of armed self-defense. That is, if anyone attacked their members, it would be all right for the members to fight back with weapons. By late 1966, James Forman, who had led SNCC's office almost since its beginning, wrote a paper in which he declared his organization had reached "rock bottom." The civil rights movement had changed, he said, but SNCC hadn't.

Both SNCC and CORE engaged in bitter internal fights over another serious issue: their own racial makeup. Both groups, which had come into existence as interracial organizations that welcomed the participation of anyone who wanted to help, regardless of color, now became all-black. They forced their white members out. The purges were very painful, especially for the most dedicated workers, like Bob Zellner, SNCC's first white field secretary, who had risked his life for the Movement (and almost lost it) a number of times and who now was being told that he was no longer wanted. The saddest part was that few of SNCC's black activists came to Zellner's defense. The agony was almost as bad at CORE.

SNCC's leadership, which previously had been Southern in background, now was made up more of Northern activists. These people had less feeling than their predecessors for the black Southern church and for its valuable contribution to the Movement. They had not been on hand for the sit-ins or for the intense preparation in the philosophy and practice of nonviolence that preceded those demonstrations. They also were less interested in the old Southern ideal of a region where blacks and whites could share power and work for progress together. Their feelings were expressed in an organizing cry, "Black Power." To one way of thinking, the term seemed perfectly reasonable. After all, the nation had been run under "White Power" for centuries; it shouldn't hurt for blacks to exercise some power now. But to many people, the phrase was as scary as the term *Black Panther party* had been in Lowndes County, Alabama. Some of the whites who had been friends of the struggle started moving away from it.

In other organizations involved in the struggle, there was far less change. At SCLC, Martin Luther King, Jr., never changed his stand in favor of nonviolence. Nor did the National Association for the Advancement of Colored People abandon its traditional role of encouraging voter registration, working for school desegregation, and bringing important lawsuits in the courts to force segregation to end.

The world had recognized the heroic work of Martin Luther King, Jr., in 1964 by honoring him with the Nobel Peace Prize. Now Dr. King moved into new territory by declaring, in 1967, his opposition to the war in Vietnam. Dr. King had been critical before of the U.S. government for sending its troops halfway around the world to protect a foreign government while refusing to insure the safety of its own citizens at home when they tried to exercise their constitutional rights. The leader was widely criticized for bringing up the subject of Vietnam. Even some of his fellow civil rights leaders scolded him. They said he should pay attention only to what was going on at home. To Dr. King, peace was peace, regardless of where it was sought. His position lost him, and the Movement, more sympathizers.

Dr. King and others who stayed with the Movement after Selma had a lot of hard work ahead of them. The struggle for economic justice—fairness in the workplace, an end to poverty, support for the millions of poor families in the nation—suddenly seemed a lot larger and tougher than ever. The problems seemed as formidable now as desegregated schoolrooms, lunch counters, and voting places had seemed a few years before.

But the heroes of the Movement kept on working. Where before, they had battled segregation in the dusty county seats of the South, they now took the struggle to the urban ghettoes of the North. Where before, they had marched down to the courthouse, they now walked to the legislature committee room and the negotiation table. The job of organizing—of explaining to people that changes for the better will occur in their lives if they get together and use their power wisely—continued. Martin Luther King, Jr., was in Memphis, Tennessee, helping a union of city garbage collectors get better working conditions when, on April 4, 1968, he was assassinated by a hidden gunman. Eventually a white segregationist was arrested and convicted of the crime.

The Movement didn't end. A lot of the people who had signed up for the fight against discrimination back in the fifties, after the *Brown* decision, or in the sixties, after Montgomery or Greensboro or the Freedom Ride or Birmingham or Danville or Selma, kept on marching—as a Movement song put it, "marching down to freedom land."

They were, as they had been back in the beginning, ordinary people—tall, short, male, female, fat, skinny, dark-skinned, light-skinned, extremely intelligent and just medium—who had been on hand when history needed them. There were thousands of them. The stories of a few of them are told on the following pages. It's important to remember that they were just ordinary people—and that they were all heroes.

SEVEN

Growing Up in Mississippi: Joyce Ladner

Joyce Ladner's mother and father were living in Hattiesburg, a city in southeastern Mississippi, when the time came for Joyce to be born. In was 1943, and it was not unusual back then for women to return to their family homes to have their babies. So Joyce, the third of what were to be nine children, was born in a little community named Battles, down near Mississippi's Gulf of Mexico coast. Not long afterward, the family moved to a tiny all-Negro community near Hattiesburg called Palmer's Crossing. Neither that community nor Battles are big enough to appear on the official Mississippi state highway map today.

The area around Palmer's Crossing was less of an oppressive, mean place in terms of race relations than were other parts of Mississippi—the Delta, for instance. The Delta is a flat stretch of rich soil that runs along the Mississippi River for some two hundred miles, from Vicksburg, Mississippi, to Memphis, Tennessee. Because of the nutrients brought by the river, the Delta was ideal for producing cotton. Since cotton required a lot of labor to grow and pick, a large black population was required to work on the cotton plantations. Racial discrimination was at its strongest in Mississippi's Delta.

Palmer's Crossing was different from the Delta. People had farms around Palmer's Crossing, but they were nowhere near plantation-sized. There was some small-time manufacturing, and during World War II, many people worked in jobs at a nearby military camp. Black women often worked as maids and cooks in the homes of better-off white families, and black men worked in various trades. Joyce Ladner's father was an automobile mechanic.

When she was growing up, Ladner says today, "I had an acute sense of being oppressed" by racism. She didn't really know how well off she was until she visited the Delta when she was a teenager, but there was oppression enough back at home. "One of my earliest recollections," she says, "is of walking past the public library and not being able to go into it. And it was getting used textbooks each year. That still makes me upset."

The schoolbooks that Joyce Ladner received had obviously been used by other students—white students—before they were handed over to Joyce and other black children. That was a tradition in much of the Deep South. "They had the names in them," said Ladner, "and I used to wonder what Sue Bell Jones looked like. Was she a smart girl like me? Or what does Johnny Jackson look like? And what are his interests?"

Joyce would play games—take part in imaginary conversations with the children who had used those books before. "They were part of my world," she says, "but they *weren't*. They were daily reminders; every time I opened that book, I saw their names. And also I knew that they had used them until they were in a state of disrepair, and then I had to use them."

The books always reminded her of two disturbing things. One was her strong quest for knowledge. Joyce was a bright child, always "interested in learning," and the books represented the world outside that could be reached through education. But at the same time, the books reminded her that the people who ran the system had classified her, because of the color of her skin, as inferior, as second class.

Another event that disturbed her occurred when a new school was built in her community. It was modern and made of bricks, and it was a short distance from Joyce's house. But she couldn't go there; it was a "white" school. Joyce wondered out loud one day why she couldn't go. "My mother explained it by saying, well, that was for white kids, and it wasn't good enough for me." Still, Joyce thought, "What's wrong with *me*? Why can't they build *us* a school?"

Events such as these have occurred in the lives of many people who grew up in the segregated society, whether they were white or black. Obviously, they had more impact on black children, since the incidents seemed to ask that terrible question that confronted Joyce Ladner: "What's wrong with *me*?"

The event that Joyce Ladner recalls most clearly is one that is remembered by many African-Americans: hearing the news of the lynching of Emmett Till. It was, says Ladner, "what separated my wheat from my chaff. Emmett Till drew a line, a boundary, in my consciousness between what's absolutely right and what's absolutely wrong."

She heard about it one day through word of mouth.

Someone in the neighborhood brought the news. After that, Joyce, who was twelve, gathered all the information on the murder that she could find. She saved her nickels so she could run to the nearby grocery store and get a copy of the *Hattiesburg American* when it arrived at 4:20 each afternoon. She would buy the paper and run back home. She clipped out articles about the case and pasted them in a scrapbook. She remembers being at a friend's house one day, "lying on the floor and reading these articles about this poor boy. I remember crying a lot about what happened to him, and I remember feeling very, very vulnerable. Mine was the Emmett Till generation. I'll never forget how horrible I felt, and the powerlessness. I remember crying a lot about this boy. It was as if it had happened to *me*." The murdered youth had been only two years older than Joyce.

Four years later, she cried again, this time for Mack Charles Parker, who was lynched in Poplarville, about twenty miles away.

Parker had been arrested and accused of assaulting a white woman. Ladner was convinced that when he and his lawyer got into court, they would be able to make the judge and jury believe Parker's statement that he had been somewhere else at the time, and they would set him free. "I was *so* optimistic that once they get to court, he's got the facts, and the facts are going to prevail," she said. But on the night before the trial, a lynch mob came and took Parker away and killed him.

"I'll never forget how terrified I was that this could happen to my brothers and my father and the men I knew," said Ladner. After the lynching, members of the press converged on Hattiesburg to write the story of what had happened. Joyce and her sister, Dory, went to Hattiesburg to see the spectacle. They were especially fascinated by the reporters from foreign publications. "These were foreign correspondents, and they spoke a foreign language. And we used to stand on the corner and pretend that we were speaking a foreign language. It was our way of saying, 'One day we won't be in these conditions.' We always had these dreams of being in faraway places."

These awful moments created a fiery anger in Joyce Ladner, and she promised herself that "one day, I'm going to get even with these people who did this." They also convinced the young woman that truly evil people actually did exist.

"There was evil in the world," she said. "And I had the sense that, 'One day when I get real big'—meaning grown—'I'm going to go away and get education.' When someone would ask me, 'What are you going to be when you grow up?' I'd say, 'I just want to get an education so I can help people.'" She didn't know the expression *social worker* at the time, but she thinks now that's what she meant. Dory, her sister, wanted to be a lawyer. The feminist movement had not spread its influence widely then, and Joyce Ladner expressed her dreams not in terms of herself, but of the sons she hoped to have someday. "I always said I wanted to have four sons," she said. "One would be the first black U.S. senator; one would be the governor; one would be a doctor; and I don't remember what the other one would be—maybe a lawyer. This was before feminism, and I had the sense that my power would come through having these sons who would change things."

The Ladners had a family friend, a man named Dr.

McLeod, who frequently reminded Joyce and her sister that *they* were the "new generation" and that they had an obligation to improve society. "He was an herb doctor," Ladner recalls. "We called him 'Cousin.' He brought the *Pittsburgh Courier* and all the other publications to us, and also lots of books about black history. He was in the local NAACP chapter, and he admonished Dory and me all the time: 'You girls have a responsibility to change these things.' He was a true mentor. I felt that it was just a matter of time; that one day all of this is going to change, and I'm going to have some role in it."

Joyce's horizon widened when people at her church who were active in NAACP activities invited her to go with them to Jackson, Mississippi's capital and largest city, to attend statewide NAACP meetings. There she met the courageous Medgar Evers and, once when he visited Mississippi, Roy Wilkins, the executive director of the national organization.

In the fall of 1960, Joyce and Dory Ladner entered Jackson State College (now Jackson State University) in the capital. The college, which was run by the state government, had strict rules about students' (particularly the females) leaving the campus. But the sisters would frequently sign out for shopping trips downtown and go instead to Medgar Evers's NAACP office to help out. One day (it was after February 1, 1960, when the Greensboro sit-ins started) Evers told the girls a secret: There was going to be a sit-in at the Jackson Public Library by students from Tougaloo College, a nearby church-supported school.

The sisters wanted to take part in the demonstration. But Evers cautioned them that they would surely be expelled from Jackson State if they did. They couldn't tell the college officials that they were leaving the campus to go to the downtown library because black people weren't allowed in the library. But if they signed out to go shopping and went to the demonstration instead and were arrested or were otherwise brought to the college's attention, they would be expelled from school.

Evers told the sisters there were other ways they could help, however. "He said we *could* organize the students," Ladner recalled. And that is what the sisters did. They secretly spread the word of the demonstration on the campus. When the day of the sit-in came, they skipped class and stayed in their dormitory room, listening to the radio. When they heard that the students had been arrested, their plan went into action: The Ladners promoted a sympathy demonstration on the campus, at the Jackson State library. The college president, who owed his job to the state, was extremely upset, and the authorities brought police dogs to the campus to stop the meeting.

On the next day, the situation was even more tense. Police officers covered the campus, and when Jackson State students announced they were going to march downtown to the courthouse, where the Tougaloo students were being brought into court, the police turned dogs and tear gas on them.

The Ladner sisters left Jackson State at the end of that school year (if they hadn't, they probably would have been asked to leave) and entered Tougaloo. The church-operated school was completely different from Jackson State. "I felt like I'd died and gone to heaven," said Joyce later. It was at Tougaloo that she met many of the leaders of the young protest movement that was being started. "It was a free environment," she said. "For all of my life I had known that there was something wrong—that I couldn't think and say what I wanted to. I couldn't express myself. Now, for the first time, I said, 'This is incredible! I can say what I want to! I can think the thoughts that I have and not feel that there's something wrong with them!' It was just the most wonderful feeling."

Joyce Ladner thinks that black young people all over the South made similar discoveries and that those young people—who at first didn't know one another or even know that there were others out there who felt the same way—formed "a foundation" for the Movement that was to follow.

While she was at Tougaloo, Ladner got to know organizers from the Student Nonviolent Coordinating Committee. Since SNCC didn't demand that its members work full-time (the pay for a field secretary was ten dollars a week, before taxes, so few people could *afford* to work exclusively for SNCC), it was easy for Ladner and her sister to combine going to school with trying to change society. Because of her and other students, Tougaloo became known as an important Mississippi outpost for the Movement. When ministers would travel from the North to Jackson to try to desegregate white churches in Mississippi, they would stop first at Tougaloo. Ladner helped to convince performers—singers, musicians, actors—that they should not take part in Mississippi events that were segregated.

She wrote speeches for SNCC officials, and she helped publish a newsletter that went to Northern friends of the civil rights group. Ladner thinks she never reached her full potential as a student because she was juggling so much Movement work. But in her mind, the Movement was terribly important, and it made the academic losses worthwhile. There were many college students back then who felt the same way. They knew that the Movement was a once-in-a-lifetime thing and that it was worthwhile to set their studies aside for a few years. In many cases, including Joyce Ladner's, people did return full-time to school after their time in the Movement was over.

"The core group in SNCC was the full-time organizers," said Ladner, "like my sister Dory. I always say she was the heroine of the movement. She's the one who went into Natchez [where there was a violent confrontation with segregationists] and got shot at and everything." But there was also that other group of student activists on the campuses—the group to which Joyce Ladner belonged.

"There was a lot of overlap, too. We would go out and canvass for the registered voters. I could take a group of students from the campus and go into Jackson, or take them up to Greenwood or Greenville or down to Hattiesburg or Laurel or any of these massive Movement projects we had. We went to Atlanta for all the SNCC conferences, and we came to Howard University. But I always did define my role differently than those people who had dropped out of school and worked full time."

Ladner participated with SNCC in the Freedom Summer project of 1964, and after that, she left the state to go to graduate school in St. Louis, Missouri. She took part in civil rights demonstrations and organizing there, and she made frequent trips back to Mississippi. But she felt guilty about not being there where the danger was, where her sister was.

When the two were little children, Dory Ladner used

91

to take up for her sister. "When someone hit me," recalled Joyce, "she would hit them back for me." Now, when she was in St. Louis, Joyce would often call her sister, back in the thick of Movement activity in Mississippi.

"I'd call," said Joyce, "and she'd say, 'They just shot at our house.' I would feel awful. My sister and I were very, very close, all our lives. And you cannot imagine how awful I felt that I was in the safe haven of graduate school, trying to study, and she was getting shot at.

"I had these two things tugging at me, pulling at me. There was always this war inside me: one, wanting to get this education, and the other, wanting to be part of the Movement. So I played both these things together; I never made a choice of one over the other."

Ladner said she was surprised when, years after the Movement, she talked with fellow activists and learned that many of them did not believe as strongly in nonviolence as she did. They accepted nonviolence as a strategy, but not as a personal philosophy. "In my heart, I always believed in it. It was a philosophy. I believed that somehow justice would reign if I acted in a certain way—that if I comported myself in a proper way, if I didn't strike back, I felt that there was some redemption to be gained. I truly did believe that good triumphed over evil.

"I also believed in the power of reason. I believed in the power of education, and in information, and in informing people. I believed people made rational decisions, based on the information available to them. That's why I believed Mack Charles Parker's lawyer would be able to persuade a jury that this man was, indeed, elsewhere, and that he would get off. The sinister, darker side of human nature never occurred to me. I just felt that you can reason your way out of anything; that enlightenment will prevail."

Joyce Ladner's faith in the power of reason was severely shaken by some of the things that segregationists did in the Movement years. She lost some of that faith. But she didn't lose all. She went on to become an educator, and today she is a vice president of Howard University, one of the schools that has furnished so much leadership for America.

EIGHT

"Troublemakers" in the Delta: June Johnson

All over Mississippi and everyplace else in the South, young black people such as Joyce and Dory Ladner were growing up in segregation, like their parents and grandparents before them. And, just like their ancestors, they were angry at the system that they saw around them. As their parents and grandparents had done before them, they vowed to try to change the system. But these young people had a great advantage: Since their parents' day, the Movement had changed significantly. It had gained strength from court decisions and from the demonstrations at Montgomery and Greensboro and Birmingham and Albany. It had gotten strength, too, from the violence that bigots often used against the Movement. Already, some victories were being won, and discrimination was being beaten down. It was a dangerous and frustrating time in which to live, but it was also incredibly exciting.

June Johnson was born around Christmastime in 1947 in Greenwood, Mississippi, in the cotton plantation country of the Delta. Her mother was a maid and a cook in the homes and businesses of white people. Her father worked at what was called the cotton compress. Workers on the plantations would cultivate (or "chop") and pick the cotton, pulling what they picked along behind them in huge burlap bags that would sometimes weigh more than a hundred pounds. Then the cotton would go to the gin, a machine that separated the cotton fibers from the seeds and waste material. After that, June Johnson's father and others would bind the cotton into large bundles. Then the cotton would be shipped to factories that would turn the fiber into the fabric of shirts, dresses, and handkerchiefs.

Both June's mother and father often had to leave June and her six sisters and five brothers with June's grandmother while they travelled to other parts of the South to work. It was hard for Negroes in Mississippi to make a decent living then, but the Johnsons worked hard. "We really thought we were living a good life," said June Johnson not long ago. "We were clean, we were honorable, we were church-going people. We *worked*. I remember the time we worked twelve and thirteen hours a day for two dollars and fifty cents, all day long. I used to see my grandmother pull five hundred and six hundred pounds of cotton a day."

And June saw other things that made her resent the segregated system and the economic inequality that it represented. "I used to see my mother wash white women's underwear," she said. "That made me angrier than anything else. She did it before she cooked our breakfast. And she would make their biscuits before we got our breakfast. I resented that worse than anything in the world."

As it did with so many other young people of that time,

the lynching of Emmett Till left a permanent mark on June Johnson. June was eight years old. The murder had taken place about ten miles from June's home.

"People never got over that, even to this day," she says. "It was a breaking point for me. It was talked about in our house by the grown-ups, and we were told not to talk about it." June's parents tried to protect her and her sisters and brothers from possible harm by instructing them never to tell white people what their true feelings were about race relations. They figured, on the basis of a lot of evidence, including that of the Till lynching, that much harm could come to Negroes who whites thought were too outspoken, or "uppity."

"My mother used to say to me, 'If they come and ask you about integration, you're not interested in going to school with them,'" recalled Johnson. "'You say no, you're not interested in going to school with whites.'"

People who knew June also knew that she was not afraid to speak her mind, and that if a white child pushed her around, she would push right back. "My sisters used to say that I didn't have fear in me," she said. Her mother told June she wanted her to get a college education so she could get out of Greenwood. "You and these white folks aren't going to get along together here," she told June.

Even when she kept her mouth shut, June could easily see what went on beneath the surface of race relations in the Delta. Many white people there, and in other parts of the South, would defend the segregated way of life by saying that black people liked things that way, and that the races really did get along well; they just preferred to be separate. But June and her family lived at the end of a street near the railroad tracks, and they saw things from a different angle. Often, rough white people would come to the end of the street to settle their disputes among themselves, with fists and knives, out of sight of the rest of the white community. And white men would come around looking for black women. Although the most out-spoken white segregationists would shout long and hard about how segregation must keep blacks and whites apart so they would not be romantically attracted to each other, members of the black community could see with their own eyes that not all whites believed in this rule. Sometimes it was the loud-talking segregationists who came around looking for companionship.

June also saw cruelty and sudden danger. One Fourth of July, when her family had gathered at June's house to celebrate the holiday, her brother went to the neighbor-hood grocery store, which was run by a white man, to buy some grapes and a package of bubble gum. Soon the child ran back to the house. The grocer's son, a grown man, was chasing him.

"He said that my brother did not address him, a white man, properly," said June. "He said that when he asked my brother, 'Is that all?' my brother said, 'Yes.' " June's brother had made the mistake of not saying, "Yes, *sir*."

As he spoke, said June, the white man had his hand on the child, who was struggling to get loose. Only the low fence around the Johnson yard kept them apart. June's grandmother jumped up from her seat on the porch and went to investigate.

"My grandmother *lived* for us," said Johnson. "She would have laid down her life for any one of us. She kept a knife wrapped in a pocket handkerchief in her pocket. She never left her home without it. And she pulled it out and threatened to kill this man."

The children ran into the kitchen and got their mother,

who separated everybody and calmed things down. The owner of the store came and apologized for his son's behavior. But June's grandmother told the members of the family they must never patronize that store again. From that moment on, June's father bought the family's groceries from a store across town. Sometimes the merchant would deliver the food in a truck, and sometimes members of the family would walk several miles to get it.

Black people in much of the South in the fifties and sixties were usually the victims of segregation, but there was one important area where they could resist the system: They could withhold their money from it. That's what happened in Montgomery during the bus boycott (which cost the segregated bus company and downtown stores a lot of money). It happened as a result of the sit-ins (stores such as Woolworth's were under great pressure not to offend their black customers). And it happened in Greenwood when June Johnson's family stopped shopping at that neighborhood grocery store.

When the organizers from the Student Nonviolent Coordinating Committee came to Greenwood and began handing out leaflets about freedom and voter registration, June Johnson was naturally curious. And when she was walking to school in the morning, she would see Bob Moses, a SNCC field secretary, standing on the street, and they would say "Hello" to each other.

June's family knew SNCC was in Greenwood, too. "I had heard from them that these 'troublemakers' were in town," said June. "My family would whisper about it." The organizers worked out of a little office that they called Freedom House. In every community where SNCC started a campaign in the Movement years, there was a Freedom House. One morning, as she walked to school, June asked Moses: "Is it true that you're a troublemaker?"

"And he laughed," she recalled. "He said, 'No.' He changed the conversation into my going to school. He turned around and walked me to school. He was talking to me, asking me questions about Greenwood and how conditions were, and my family, how long I had lived there, and everything. We had this conversation all the way to school. He carried my books. I had never had that type of treatment. Bob would watch me get in the schoolhouse door, and I would come back to the door, and we would wave to each other."

That sort of friendliness was welcome to June. "I guess that was something that I needed," she said. "Because the way I was brought up, all I did was work. Worked, went to school, and went to church. It was a different type of exposure to kindness.

"And when the school bell would ring in the afternoon, I would tell my girlfriend, 'I'm going to stop by this Freedom place. Why don't you go with me?' And I would see Bob Moses again."

Before long, June Johnson was helping out with voter registration work.

In April of 1963, when she was sixteen, she attended a SNCC conference in Atlanta. Bob Moses arranged for June to stay with a woman who was a respected Movement activist, but even then June's mother was reluctant for her to go. She feared her daughter would be involved in some sort of trouble.

There was no trouble, though. There were about sixty members of SNCC on hand, along with about three hundred and fifty young people from around the South, as well as friends of the Movement from the North and elsewhere. June heard talks about voter registration, and she sang freedom songs, but the most remarkable thing was that she saw black people *and* white people who were working, planning, singing, and enjoying life together. "I had never seen that before," she said.

The group asked June to get up and give a report on conditions in Greenwood. She was afraid of public speaking, but she gave the report anyway. She discovered that she liked it. In fact, she liked the whole life of the Movement. "It was like being converted," she said.

Bob Moses spoke at the meeting, too. He said that the organizers in Greenwood had found that many people who wanted to register to vote were not allowed to do so because they could not read and write. The law at that time required citizens to be literate in order to register. The system, said Moses, should not refuse illiterate people the right to vote when it was the very same system that failed to make them literate in the first place. He said Greenwood was the center of activity for five counties in the Mississippi Delta, and that if a voter registration project could be a success there, "then that will crack the heart of the Delta."

The trouble that June Johnson's mother feared came two months later, when June attended another Movement meeting. This time it was in South Carolina. The meeting had been a success—June learned details of black history she never would have been taught in the public schools of Greenwood—and when it was over, she and others from Mississippi started home by bus. One of the travellers was

Fannie Lou Hamer, a forty-five-year-old woman who had joined SNCC the year before. Mrs. Hamer was the youngest of twenty children in a family from Ruleville, Mississippi, who worked as sharecroppers. (In sharecropping, a tenant family did the farming on land owned by someone else. The owner lent the sharecropper money to buy seed and equipment and to spend on family living expenses. At the end of the season, the tenant received a share of the income from the harvest, minus the money that was borrowed. Few sharecroppers ever made much money at this, and many were perpetually in debt.)

Mrs. Hamer did not know, until the Movement came, that black Americans have a right to vote. One day in 1962, she left the plantation where she worked and went to her county seat to try to register. When she returned, the plantation owner heard about what she had done, and he threw her off the land. As the Movement years wore on, Mrs. Hamer became a real legend in the struggle for freedom.

The trouble in 1963 started in Columbus, Mississippi, when the travelers—June Johnson, Fannie Lou Hamer, and the others—transferred from one bus line to another and tried to get served at the bus terminal's lunch counter. The driver clearly did not like the group. His attitude got worse when June and the others insisted on sitting wherever they wanted in the bus. In each small town where the bus stopped, the driver would go off and talk to local people. He was obviously talking about the group. "We pretty much knew that we were in trouble," recalls Johnson.

When the bus got to Winona, a town in the center of Mississippi that was about twenty-five miles from Greenwood, police cars were there. "It was a mob there, waiting," said Johnson. The group had planned to visit the lunch counter in Winona to see if the operators of the bus terminal were obeying the federal law that outlawed transportation discrimination, but when Johnson and the others sat down, the police, including Mississippi highway patrolmen, pushed them off their stools and forced them outside.

Soon the group was on its way to the jail in Winona. The police were becoming more and more abusive, and once they got to the jail, they started beating their prisoners. Fannie Lou Hamer was beaten severely. Her assailants pulled her dress over her head and clubbed her repeatedly. June Johnson was also beaten. "The highway patrolman hit me with a billy stick," she remembers. "I had on a pink dress. A beautiful pink dress, and a black scarf. And I had a bag that my mother had given me with some clothes in it. And the next thing I knew, all these police officers started beating me." The police even made black male prisoners beat the women.

"They threatened to kill us that night," said Johnson. The police, she said, pointed a gun at members of the group and told them to sign statements saying, falsely, "that we had beat each other up and that they had not done anything to us. We tried to get medical attention, and they wouldn't even give us that."

Eventually, the group got out of jail and told its story to the world. A year later, when the Mississippi Freedom Democratic party tried to get representation at the 1964 Democratic National Convention in Atlantic City, Fannie Lou Hamer was asked to testify before a party committee on this sort of "justice" in Mississippi. In a session that was televised to the nation, she told a moving story of the beatings. Her testimony was so damaging to Mississippi's "regular" Democrats, who were arguing against Freedom party representation, that President Lyndon Johnson tried to blunt the impact of Hamer's appearance by holding a quickly arranged press conference while the testimony was going on. The president managed to pull the television cameras away from the testimony, but the nation still learned what had gone on in Winona, Mississippi, and lots of other places.

June Johnson now lives in Washington, D.C., where she has served as an employee of the District of Columbia city government. She was, and still is, bitter about what happened to her and the others in Winona. "Winona is something that will never go away in my mind," she says. She thinks the civil rights organizations most closely involved—SNCC and SCLC—didn't move quickly enough to protest the beatings or to protect those who were attacked. She is not particularly happy about the way the U.S. Department of Justice acted, either. The department filed a lawsuit over the Winona case, but it lost.

But there were some positive outcomes as well. As a result of what happened in Winona, June Johnson's family became much more active in the Movement. Her mother practically turned her home into a SNCC Freedom House. And Winona made Johnson a lifelong Movement activist.

"It made me stronger," she says. "It made me more determined."

NINE

Getting Out the Vote in Mississippi: Leslie McLemore

A bout a hundred miles to the north of June Johnson's home, but still very much in Mississippi, a young man named Leslie McLemore was born in 1940 and was growing up as the Movement was evolving all around him.

Leslie was born in Walls, a small town just south of the Tennessee-Mississippi state line. Memphis, the growing and busy Tennessee city on the Mississippi River, was not far from Walls, but McLemore's hometown managed to retain its rural atmosphere. It was "a small farming community," as Leslie McLemore remembers it, "a town essentially owned by one or two men who were the large plantation owners."

McLemore's situation was quite a bit different from June Johnson's, however: His family did not have to depend on white people for their economic or social welfare. They did not have to worry about offending a plantation owner or employer. His grandfather owned land, which he used for farming, and he also ran a restaurant and participated in an occupation that was a common one in Mississippi—bootlegging. (Officially, the state outlawed the sale of alcoholic beverages. But in virtually every town or city or crossroads in the state, someone could be found who could provide the banned substance for a price. Law enforcement people rarely interfered with this bootlegging, as it is called, and some of them were personally involved in the activity.) The grandfather's enterprises gave him and the family a layer of insulation from some of the harsher effects of segregation.

Once, when Leslie's younger brother decided that he wanted to attend the Catholic church in Walls, some of the church's white members objected. Some even let it be known that the young man had caused so much trouble that he should leave town for his own safety.

"My grandfather was one of the biggest taxpayers in the town," said McLemore, "and he said no way was anybody going to threaten him by telling his grandson what to do. He said, 'You do anything you want to do. You're protected by the Constitution. And if you go to jail, I'm going to get you out.' My grandfather was an institution in that town, and they simply didn't interfere with him." The grandfather, whose name was Leslie also, had money in three banks. When he bought a new car, which he did every three years, he paid cash. When a black person got put in jail on a Saturday, the grandfather would get him out, using only his word for bail. "He was the buffer in the black community," said his grandson.

The result, says McLemore, was a relationship between whites and the members of his family that had some of the features of racism that could be found all over the South. But that racism was softened a bit by the respect that the whites had for the family. The relationship, he said, "was unequal, but it was an understanding."

Leslie McLemore could see people all around him in the black community who did not have the luxury of independence that his family enjoyed. Black people who worked for segregationist whites, or who depended on loans from white-owned banks to keep their businesses or farms going, could not afford to speak out when they saw racial injustice. The young man was especially saddened, and angered as well, when he saw his schoolteachers decline, because of fear, to say what was on their minds. In Walls, as in the rest of the South then, the schools were all-white or all-black, but the black teachers and administrators who worked in the black schools were hired and fired by whites. A teacher who spoke out about race could be forced to look for another job.

In McLemore's county, DeSoto, a high school for black students didn't even exist until 1955. Everybody knew that the school was built in response to the *Brown* decision, to keep blacks from demanding admission to the white school. When Leslie entered the school, it had a brand-new chemistry laboratory, but there was no equipment in it. There was a new library, but it held only a few books. And the textbooks that black students got were hand-me-downs from white kids, just as they had been at Joyce Ladner's school.

Les McLemore saw these things, and he wished that his teachers and principals would complain about the injustice. He saw, too, that when teachers or school officials *did* speak out, "They were fired from their jobs." The upshot, he said, was that "the most educated people in the black community could not participate" in the political process. They were afraid to try to register and vote, and they were afraid to express their opinions on political matters.

But not all of them were afraid. McLemore recalls that some of his teachers would get their messages across in ways that were indirect and that could not easily be challenged by their white supervisors. It was a technique that went back to slavery times, when the songs spoke of "crossing the River Jordan" and other things that could be interpreted in more than one way. "They would talk about citizenship," he said. "They would talk about how you're either a first-class citizen or you're a second-class citizen. And how if you aren't registered to *vote*, you're a *second*-class citizen. And how it was *necessary* to be a *first*-class citizen."

If a representative of the segregationist society was listening, he or she could hardly object to such talk about first-class citizenship. But the message that directly challenged that segregationist society was clear: Get out and register to vote, and then vote.

McLemore finished high school and went on to Rust College, in Holly Springs, Mississippi, a few miles from Walls. There he found teachers who were less shy about speaking out on race relations and other controversial issues. And he and his classmates were inspired by what was going on elsewhere. McLemore entered Rust in 1960, as the sit-in movement was sweeping over much of the South. When a student chapter of the National Association for the Advancement of Colored People was founded at Rust in 1962, McLemore was elected president. Medgar Evers, the state NAACP secretary, came from Jackson to install McLemore.

Even before that, McLemore and other Rust students participated in a boycott of a segregated movie theater in Holly Springs. Negroes were allowed to attend the theater, but they had to purchase their tickets and then climb stairs to a segregated section. The boycotters stayed away from the theater from 1960 to 1961, until the business finally desegregated.

At first, recalls McLemore, the theater operator suggested some changes that did *not* include letting people sit wherever they wanted. "They said they would extend the hours," he said, "and they would have better quality movies, and they would give college students a reduction in ticket prices—anything but opening it up so you could sit any place you wanted to." But in the end, the theater ended its seating segregation. McLemore thinks the reason was economic: Rust was one of two black colleges in the town. The colleges had a combined enrollment of about twelve hundred students. A large part of the theater's income came from black students. This was an economic lesson that would be learned during Movement years by merchants across the South.

In 1962, McLemore met Bob Moses of the Student Nonviolent Coordinating Committee. Moses had been on a visit to Rust College, and he invited McLemore to a SNCC meeting in Atlanta—just as he had done with June Johnson. By now, McLemore thought of himself as a Movement person. He continued his work with the NAACP student chapter, but more of his work was done through SNCC.

Moses, said McLemore, was talking about the need for voter registration. "And this is what we students were doing in Holly Springs. The difference is that Moses was talking about a *system* for doing it. He was talking about large-scale voter registration, where you organize a large group of people and take them all down to the courthouse. You make everybody feel better about it because you have a large group." In other words, there was safety in numbers. If an individual black man or woman went down to the courthouse to register, he or she might easily be intimidated or threatened. But if a group of people sought to exercise their basic right at the same time, it might be harder for the guardians of segregation to reject or intimidate them.

Until SNCC came along, said McLemore, "I had been lone-wolfing it. I had been out on the street, going door-to-door, telling people about voter registration; talking to them about the Constitution. And I would go back the next day. They'd say, 'Well, I'll meet you down at the courthouse.' And I would go down there, and nobody would show up.

"Occasionally I'd get a person to show up, and I'd take them in to the registrar's office." This happened enough times so that Les McLemore soon became well known among the whites at the courthouse. "I became identified over time as the guy who was causing this problem." At first, white workers at the courthouse were courteous to McLemore and the person he was helping to register. But as time passed, courtesy turned into coldness, and coldness turned into resentment, and finally Les was chased out of the county building. The group approach, as advocated by SNCC and other civil rights organizations, began to look attractive.

As the young student met other SNCC workers and learned from them about what was going on elsewhere in the Movement, he became more and more inspired. Like June Johnson, he had an opportunity during trips to Atlanta and other Movement outposts to see white and black people working together. And he was "talking to people who had common interests."

At the same time, Les McLemore was revising his thinking about what he would do when he got older. All along, he had planned to go to medical school. He wanted to make a lot of money. Then his exposure to the Movement made him think he perhaps should enter law school. Lawyers, after all, were playing an important role. They were winning victories not only for the Movement, but also for people who lacked the strength or ability to become active in the Movement but who nevertheless benefitted from the struggle's successes. Schoolchildren and ordinary bus riders might never take part in a demonstration, but they could surely take advantage of a desegregation order that was won in a federal courtroom by a skilled civil rights attorney.

There was some pressure, too, not to continue his education at all after he finished at Rust College. Many of the Movement's activists had made that decision. In fact, quite a few of them had dropped out of college, or never even began it, so they could spend all their time on Movement activities.

But Les McLemore thought some more, and he decided that he should be neither a doctor nor a lawyer, but rather a teacher. A good friend of his reminded him that the serious problems of discrimination would still be around long after he graduated from college and that he owed it to others to help them get an education, too. Because of the emphasis his parents and grandparents had placed on education, "school was sacred to me," he says. So when he finished at Rust in 1964, McLemore went to Atlanta University, where he received a graduate degree in political science. Then he got his doctorate in government from the University of Massachusetts and came back to Mississippi to teach.

Before he left Rust, though, McLemore took part in one of the Movement's more interesting—and frustrating—moments. In the summer of 1964, he was selected as a delegate from the Mississippi Freedom Democratic party (MFDP) to the Democratic National Convention in Atlantic City, New Jersey. As was explained in chapter 5, the MFDP challenged the national party's seating of the "regular" Mississippi delegation on the grounds that the party in that state practiced segregation and worked to deny black people their right to vote.

There was some controversy over how the MFDP, which was controlled by SNCC, selected its delegates to the national convention. SNCC had always made the point that local people should decide their own future and that it would be wrong for an outside organization, even SNCC, to try to impose its will on those local people. So, in theory, local Mississippians would name their delegates to Atlantic City. In actuality, SNCC's field secretaries did a lot of the selecting beforehand, and some of the delegates were more in the category of "civil rights organizer" than "local person."

Les McLemore was one of those who was definitely local, despite the fact that he had worked with SNCC. When the delegates were being selected, he said, someone suggested that he be chosen. "They said, 'We have Leslie McLemore, straight from Mississippi.' They said, 'Speak,

McLemore.' And once I started talking, there was no question about it. They said, 'Yeah, he's from Mississippi.' " (McLemore has a pronounced Mississippi accent.) He was selected, along with sixty-three other blacks and four whites, to take the challenge to the national convention.

McLemore, as well as most of the others who carried the struggle from Mississippi to Atlantic City, was deeply disappointed by the national party's refusal to recognize their claim and seat the nonsegregationist group, despite the moving testimony of Fannie Lou Hamer about the inequality of political participation in her home state. "You have to understand," he said not long ago, "that we went to Atlantic City with the notion that we ought to be the legitimate, recognized delegation from this state. We went there with the notion that we had God on our side, and the law on our side, and that if the nation heard our case, there was no way they could say that we were not the legitimate delegation. We were sharecroppers and a few independent landowners—essentially people who worked for other people. At great risk these people were going to Atlantic City. And we had right on our side, and we thought that we would be seated."

After the rejection at Atlantic City, Les McLemore became bitter toward the system that he had believed in for so long. But the experience had benefitted him too. He learned how to go into the offices of prominent party officials—members of Congress, many of them—and explain what his position was and why they should support it. The technique is called lobbying (from the idea that backers or opponents of certain legislation argue their cases to elected representatives in the lobbies outside the legislative chambers). It is a vital part of the American political system. Atlantic City, said McLemore, "was a real education for me."

He was able to put that education to good use in later years. After he received his degrees at Atlanta University and the University of Massachusetts, McLemore went to Jackson State University as a professor of political science. And in 1988, he went to his second Democratic National Convention. This time he was an officially selected delegate. The Mississippi Democratic party, which had chosen him, was no longer a segregated institution.

Of the delegates to the 1988 Democratic National Convention, which was held in Atlanta, almost 23 percent were black. This was the highest percentage of black representation in the history of any big-party American nominating convention, and it was a bit higher than the percentage of all blacks in the nation. Voter registration—carried out by groups of heroic organizers like Les McLemore—had changed the face of politics not only in the most segregated state in America, but in America as a whole.

TEN

Becoming an Activist:
Charles Jones

As a child in Chester, South Carolina, Charles Jones had plenty of opportunities to see segregation in action. The small textile mill town was not far from the place where South Carolina's first branch of the Ku Klux Klan was born. Although geographically South Carolina was not a Deep South state like Alabama or Mississippi, it was known far and wide as a place where segregation was strictly enforced by custom and law.

Charles was born in 1937. His mother was an English teacher in the Negro school, and his father was a minister in the Presbyterian church. Like many other black Americans, he has a clear memory of discriminatory incidents early in life. A black teacher, a colleague of his mother's, had gone into a drugstore in Chester to get a prescription filled. When the white pharmacist handed the medicine to her, she said, "Thank you." But because she did not add "Sir" to her thanks, the pharmacist slapped her in the face.

Before long, Jones's family moved to Charlotte, a larger

city just across the state line in North Carolina. Charles went away to high school, to a church-operated school in Columbia, South Carolina. He remembers being on the school's campus when he heard about the Supreme Court's decision in the case of *Brown* v. *Board of Education*, and he remembers the excitement he felt. "Schools were going to be opening up, I thought," he said later. "Society was going to be opened up. Finally we were going to develop some kind of rational society." The seventeen-year-old Charles thought that the schools would be desegregated promptly, in keeping with the court's decision. It was "just a matter of working out the details," he felt.

Charles graduated from high school and entered Johnson C. Smith University in Charlotte, where he thought he would study to become a minister like his father. All around him, the political leaders of the Southern states were showing that they were *not* going to desegregate the schools quickly. What was worse, some of them were showing that they were willing to allow segregationists to use violence to keep the schools separate. Still, Charles Jones maintained his belief that the American system would bring an end to discrimination. "I still believed the Constitution," he said, and its promise, "All men are created equal."

While Jones was in college, another important event occurred in the life of the Movement: the Montgomery bus boycott. Again, the young man was excited and made hopeful by what he saw on television: large numbers of black people—ordinary people—who had decided that they had had enough segregation and who now were walking to work rather than cooperate with a discriminatory system. And he also saw pictures of Martin Luther King,

Jr., preaching the message of the new Movement as it had never been delivered before. Charles Jones remembers those days as "not only a fresh ray of light, but just *food* for the intellect and the soul." Jones sought out books from the school library on nonviolence, on Mohandas Gandhi, and on social change.

At the same time, Charles Jones's horizons were widening in other ways. He became interested in student government at the college. That was not surprising, given his faith that the democratic system would solve the nation's problems of race relations. He became Johnson C. Smith's delegate to the North Carolina Student Legislature. Once a year, student government leaders from all over the state went to the capitol in Raleigh to play the roles of legislators. They debated important issues, held committee meetings, and "passed" bills. In the process, they gained some knowledge of how government works.

One of the ways any lawmaking body works is through compromise among the lawmakers. In Congress, in state legislatures, on county commissions and city councils, it is rare that one member gets his or her own way. Cooperation is very important. To get votes for your proposed law to raise the tax on gasoline by one cent a gallon, for example, you might have to win over a fellow legislator whose constituents are dead set against an increase. You might need to get some help from another legislator who works hard to improve education and who knows that the tax increase will go to buy more schoolbooks and pay more teachers' salaries.

In his brief stint as a "legislator," Charles Jones discovered something else. He found that there were many *white* people of his own age—student leaders at white colleges and universities—who disliked racism and segregation, too. They were hoping, as he was, that the system would soon be changed. This, too, was exciting for Jones, and it strengthened his belief that segregation would soon be over.

Jones finished Johnson C. Smith and entered the college's school of divinity. In his final year at the school, Jones got a chance to go to Europe as part of an international festival of young people. The Cold War was on everybody's minds back then. Cold War was the name for that fierce competition between democratic nations (led by the United States) and the Communist countries (led by what then was the Soviet Union). It wasn't a real war, with bombs and bullets, but international relations always seemed about to erupt into a shooting war. There was much threatening and bluffing. Some of the Communist-led countries were sending students to the festival, which was held in Vienna, Austria, as were some of the democratic countries. There was also a contingent of students from places that were not firmly committed to either democracy or communism. These included the emerging black-led nations of Africa. Both America and the Communist countries hoped to win those students over to their side. The Communists lost no opportunity to point out that America, through its system of racial segregation, was treating its own black citizens unfairly.

Charles Jones found himself debating this issue in Vienna. He told the delegates from around the world that it was correct that America had plenty of faults and that one of them was surely racism. But even with those defects, he said, his homeland was a place full of hope, a place whose citizens could peacefully change the system.

His hometown newspaper carried stories of his statements, and when he returned home to Charlotte, Jones was treated as a hero. The mayor of the city saw him on the street and congratulated him. "He told me I was a credit to my race," said Jones, with a grin. (The expression *credit to your race* was used a lot back then by well-meaning white people who apparently were unaware that they were delivering an insult. It was like saying, "Well, you may not be a credit to the *human* race, but for a black person, you're pretty good.") A committee of Congress, one that was intensely anti-Communist, invited Jones to Washington in early 1960 to testify about what he had said in Vienna.

Jones was driving home to Charlotte from Washington late one night when he heard, on his car radio, about the sit-ins in Greensboro. A handful of college students—people his own age who attended a college not all that far from his own—had walked into a Woolworth's store and sat down at the lunch counter and politely demanded to be served. And when they had been denied that service, they had stayed.

The news struck Charles Jones like a flash of light. He had the same feeling he had had back when he heard about *Brown* and the Montgomery bus bycott. Of course! The sit-in demonstration was a perfect way to strike at segregation. It was nonviolent, and it was effective. It made white society stop and think, perhaps for the first time, about the discriminatory system in which black society lived twenty-four hours a day. It was, Jones said later, "a handle" for dealing with segregation.

He hurried home, got a little sleep, and woke up early the next morning. He gathered the members of Smith's student council, of which he was vice president, and he told them he was going to have a sit-in in downtown Charlotte. He said, "Listen: Tomorrow morning, I'm going down to Woolworth's. If you want to come, fine." He had no idea how many students would want to join him.

When Jones appeared on the campus the following morning, some three hundred students were there. They were ready to march downtown. Jones was overjoyed. "I'll never forget the feeling of raw power," he said later. They filled up the lunch counters at the Woolworth's store, and then they went to the Kress's store. Jones was the chief organizer of the demonstration, and so he hurried from one store to the other to see how the protest was going. On one of his trips, he bumped into Charlotte's mayor, who, like a lot of people, had turned out to see what was happening. This was the same mayor who had congratulated Jones on his performance in Vienna.

Jones says he will never forget the way the mayor looked when he saw who was leading the sit-ins. "He looked at me with the most interesting, puzzled look on his face," he said.

After organizing the sit-ins in Charlotte, Charles Jones was a confirmed and devoted member of the Movement. He stopped being an *observer* of what was happening and started being one of those who was making it happen. He attended the meeting at Shaw University in Raleigh and helped to form the organization that soon would be called the Student Nonviolent Coordinating Committee. He met other students from other colleges who had been thinking along the same lines as he. He particularly enjoyed getting to know the students from Nashville, who were quite advanced in their study of nonviolence. It was, he recalls, "a spontaneous, exciting time."

The "spontaneous" nature of that time led the young opponents of segregation to experiment a lot. One of the experiments they tried was James Lawson's jail,-no-bail theory. Some students in Rock Hill, South Carolina, had done what students everywhere were doing—they had walked into stores and sat down at lunch counters—and they were arrested. (In some of the places where the sit-in technique was tried, as in Greensboro, the stores and the white authorities tried to ignore the students, hoping they would go away. In others, white authorities tried to help the demonstrators and store owners work out some sort of compromise. In still others, the authorities or the store owners had the students arrested and jailed on charges of "disturbing the peace" or of "unlawful public assembly" or of violating the local segregation laws. These charges were eventually thrown out by the federal courts, but sometime, the decisions came years later.)

The Rock Hill students decided to stay in jail to draw attention to their case, rather than post bond and get out while waiting for their trials. Charles Jones and other members of the newly formed SNCC went to Rock Hill to help out. They were immediately arrested, and they went to jail. A judge found them guilty and sentenced them to thirty days of work on the roads. "On the roads," in South Carolina and many other places, meant time spent doing hard work digging or clearing ditches and cutting brush alongside state or county roads. It was dangerous work. It was hot in summer and cold in winter, and there was always the danger of snakebite. A guard stood nearby, a shotgun resting on his hip, and any prisoner who tried to run stood a good chance of being shot.

Charles Jones's father came to visit him at the jail. The authorities told him he couldn't see his son. "And that old man stood there," recalled Jones not long ago, "and said, 'Well, I'm going to see my son, so do whatever you have to do.' And they let him in. And his doing that gave me a lot of inspiration." There was inspiration elsewhere, as well. All over the South, black people and sympathetic whites heard of the students' decision to go to jail—one of the places the black community feared most—and they were proud. And a little bit of their fear drained away.

The thirty days passed and Charles Jones returned to school. In May 1961, while he was taking his final examinations for the school year, he learned of CORE's Freedom Ride into Alabama. He barely finished his last exam and headed south to join the Nashville students on the second ride. Jones was arrested in Montgomery. He was getting used to the insides of jails now.

In the summer of 1961, as the nation's attention was focussed on the Freedom Rides, U.S. Attorney General Robert F. Kennedy talked with some of those who had been leading demonstrations. The attorney general was under pressure to try to end the rides, which were attracting violence that certainly didn't make America look good to the rest of the world. But he was also under pressure not to seem opposed to the demonstrators' aims. All they wanted, after all, was assurance of the rights that other Americans had; that was something the attorney general of the United States and the president (who in this case was also his brother) said they wanted, too.

Attorney General Kennedy suggested that the young

people put their energies not into demonstrations but into registering voters. If they wanted the system changed, what better way to change it than by registering people who could vote good politicians into office? (Of course, the attorney general thought that he and his brother certainly fit into the "good politician" category.)

Some of those who attended the meeting in Kennedy's office liked the idea. Charles Jones was one of them. Others feared that Kennedy was trying to exert too much control over the Movement. They believed that the Movement had to remain independent. Among those who felt this way was Diane Nash, the young student from Nashville's Fisk College who had led the second Freedom Ride.

When the meeting was over, the young people decided to do both. Some, led by Diane Nash, would continue to concentrate on what they called direct action, while others, led by Charles Jones, moved into voter registration. And where better to start their work, thought Jones and others, than in Mississippi, where less than 6 percent of the black people who were old enough to vote were registered and where in thirteen counties there were no blacks registered at all?

Jones and others from SNCC arrived in McComb, Mississippi, late in the summer of 1961. They quickly found out that in Mississippi and in other parts of the Deep South, there was no real difference between voter registration and direct action. As far as the segregationists were concerned, helping black people become registered voters *was* direct action. To them, the idea of Negroes who had the power to choose at the ballot box who would lead them was every bit as big a challenge as a confrontation at a lunch counter or at an interstate bus terminal.

Bob Moses, a young mathematics teacher from the North who had joined up with SNCC, had gone to McComb and other places in Mississippi a few months earlier. (This was the same young man who would befriend June Johnson and Les McLemore.) Moses and others who followed him set up Freedom Schools. These were clinics, usually conducted in churches, where local people could learn how to register. Mississippi and other Southern states required prospective voters to take tests to prove that they could read and write and that they knew about the operations of government. Like almost everything else in those days, the tests were not administered fairly. Black people were required to read and explain complicated sections of the state constitution—*and* to explain them to the satisfaction of the county registrar. Often, whites who wanted to vote weren't even tested at all.

The cards were definitely stacked against blacks who wanted to vote. All over the South, there were stories about Negroes who were college professors—who even taught courses in United States government or history—who were denied the right to vote. The freedom schools were an effort to do something about this situation. The SNCC people taught basic reading and writing, and they explained the state constitution, and they acquainted people with the complex form that they would be required to fill out once they went down to the courthouse.

The young organizers also did what they could to prepare local people for other, harsher forms of discrimination. They knew—and so did the local people—that political power was a terribly important thing in those Deep South counties where black people outnumbered whites. Would die-hard segregationist whites use violence to keep blacks from voting, as some of them were now

123

doing to keep the schools and bus terminals separate? The answer was not long in coming. A white state legislator shot and killed Herbert Lee, who had been active in voter registration work. The white man said he had shot in self-defense, and he was not prosecuted.

When Charles Jones and the others got to McComb, they found that a group of black high school students had tried to desegregate a lunch counter downtown and had been arrested. The new arrivals from SNCC organized a mass meeting at a local church. Jones calls it "another one of those historic mileposts for the Movement," a meeting that was full of music and singing, speechmaking, and energy—and indignation that many of the young people of the community had been put in jail.

Out of that mass meeting, the community organized a march to the courthouse, and practically everybody who went was arrested. The planners had decided that one of their number should not go, but rather should stay behind and serve as a communications link with the rest of the world. They chose Charles Jones. He felt bad about staying out of jail when everybody else was going in, but he stuck by the plan. The police tried to arrest him *anyway*, on charges that he had helped to plan the demonstration. But Jones hid from them in the back of a butcher shop in the black community. The shop was on the ground floor of the building that SNCC used as its headquarters in McComb. For years afterward, Jones was afraid to return to Mississippi because he had heard that the police had a warrant out for his arrest.

During his brief time at McComb, when he was serving as the Movement's connection with the world, Jones called the United States Department of Justice and asked for help. A Justice Department lawyer named John Doar, a man who would become known as a courageous, hard worker against discrimination, appeared one night. Jones could see that the lawyer—even though he was a representative of the United States government—was afraid in McComb. That was when Charles Jones realized that if the people who made up the Movement were going to achieve victories, they would probably have to do all the work on their own.

The federal government might pass some laws, and its courts might issue some rulings. The top-ranking political figures in Washington could be expected to give speeches about the need for violence to end and for brotherhood to reign. But when it came down to making real change, the Movement was on its own—even if that change was as simple and basic as registering people to vote.

After the time in Mississippi, Charles Jones and some other SNCC workers went to Albany, Georgia, to help with the movement there. Martin Luther King, Jr., and the SCLC were in Albany, as well as SNCC. As was explained in chapter 4, in some ways, that summer of 1962 in Albany was a defeat for the Movement. But in many others, it was a great victory.

Albany was the place where the freedom songs were sung the best. It was the place where the mass meetings were truly massive. The headquarters of the Movement in Albany was two churches, situated across the street from each other on Whitney Avenue, a pleasant street in the black community. Often when the Movement would announce a mass meeting for one of the churches, Shiloh

Baptist, so many people would turn up that a second meeting would take place afterward across the street at Mount Zion Baptist.

It was in Albany that Charles Jones changed his mind about becoming a minister. There were two reasons. For one thing, he had a chance in Albany to study closely the roles in the Movement that were played by the black community's ministers, and he felt that sometimes the ministers were acting like followers of the people, rather than their leaders.

But the other, and more important, reason was C. B. King. This man (who was not related to Martin Luther King, Jr.) was a member of a large and respected family in Albany's black community, and he was a lawyer. For much of the Movement years, he was the *only* black lawyer in southern Georgia. C. B. King was intelligent and dignified, and he could talk rings around most other lawyers. He was also absolutely fearless. More than one segregationist policeman tried to get the better of C. B. King, either inside or outside the courtroom. In one case, a sheriff bashed King's head in with a cane. The lawyer, blood gushing from his scalp, calmly sought out an FBI agent and reported the attack. The sheriff was not arrested. But King always emerged as the real winner of any dispute about segregation. Charles Jones worked closely with C. B. King, and he soon decided that he could help the world more if he forgot about becoming a preacher and became a lawyer instead.

He did become a lawyer. Jones left the Movement's front lines in the South not long after that summer in Albany and moved to New York City, where he continued to work on issues that were important to the Movement.

126

One of them was the Harlem Education Project, which sought to improve education possibilities for young blacks in New York City. He got married, and then he entered law school at Howard University in Washington, D.C. Law school can keep a student pretty busy, but even then Charles Jones stayed with the Movement. He worked with groups that were trying to end discrimination in the suburbs that surround Washington.

And he remembered "the old days." He remembered the mass meetings, and the singing of the freedom songs. "These were the songs that everybody in the black community knew," he said. "And when we put them in the context of the present struggle, and when those songs were being sung by hundreds of people in mass meetings throughout the South—there was a sort of magic that took place. All of a sudden, people were able to overcome their individual fear, and be motivated by that wave of humanity that was all around them."

And he remembers his father, who had given him so much of his own strength. Back in 1960, after the sit-ins Charles Jones had organized had been going on awhile, the merchants in downtown Charlotte agreed to desegregate their lunch counters. Finally, the lunch counters were open to everyone. Jones and his father went downtown to eat lunch. They went to a drugstore that had a lunch counter that had never been open to black people before. Jones ordered a tuna fish sandwich.

"My dad was nervous, but controlled," recalled Jones. "And I knew he was afraid. But he was very proud of me. We went in there and sat down, and I've never seen such pride in anybody in all my life as I saw in him."

ELEVEN

Black and White Together: David Crosland, Val Coleman, Constance Curry

The civil rights movement was all about securing the same rights for *all* Americans that *some* Americans had been enjoying. "All" Americans, of course, meant Americans of every skin color and ethnic background—and that, in the 1950s and 1960s, more than anything else meant Americans of African heritage. The "some" Americans who had enjoyed all along the rights of voting and self-improvement through education and had had the freedom to travel without discrimination were white people. Even some of those white people encountered discrimination part of the time: In many parts of the country, Jewish people were not welcomed in certain neighborhoods or social clubs. But by and large, the work of the Movement was to remove the segregation that white people imposed on those whose skins were darker.

It would be incorrect, however, to think of the civil rights movement as a movement only of black people. White Americans were involved in the struggle at every level except the very top. Like their fellow citizens who were black, these whites performed their work for the Movement in a great variety of ways. Some devoted practically every waking hour to toiling for an end to segregation. Some worked hard for a summer or a year or so and then returned to school or to their careers. Some volunteered for part-time work; in their spare time, they licked stamps and folded newsletters in organization offices. Some marched in the Movement's more prominent demonstrations, and others worked behind the scenes. Some were beaten by segregationists, just as blacks were beaten, and some died, just as blacks died.

When a white person came to help, one of the problems that the leaders of the Movement organizations faced had to do with "taking over." Many of those who joined the Movement had enjoyed the benefits of superior education. They were members of well-to-do families. They were articulate, which is to say they were skilled at speaking and writing and generally communicating their ideas to other people. These whites were likely to be quite successful in just about everything they did. They were accustomed, therefore, to assuming positions of leadership.

Black leaders knew that whites had a great deal to offer the Movement, but they also knew that it was important for the Movement to be controlled by black Americans themselves. They knew that segregation could not be ended until *blacks* brought it to an end; it would not work if someone else fought their battle for them. Throughout the years, one of the excuses that segregationists used to justify their system was that blacks "aren't ready" or "aren't qualified" to enjoy the same freedoms as everybody else. The segregated system, they said, was actually built to *help* and protect black people. As absurd as this argument might sound, a lot of whites accepted it. Now, in the rapidly growing years of a civil rights movement that received its inspiration, guidance, and energy from black people who were *quite* ready and qualified, its leaders didn't want to see that strength wasted.

Some of the whites who came to help had trouble adjusting to this idea, but many more of them understood. They contributed their talents, their time, and their energies to the Movement, and they did not demand control of it in return. One of the verses of the wonderful Movement anthem, "We Shall Overcome," contained the line, "Black and white together," and these whites believed in that. Often when the anthem was sung, the people who were singing it would gather in a circle and cross their arms in front of them, holding the hands of the people on either side. There were black hands and there were white hands, and they all were equal.

David Crosland

David Crosland was born in Montgomery, Alabama, in 1936, to a prominent family that was white and that believed in segregation. His father was the city attorney for Montgomery; he prosecuted Rosa Parks for her refusal to move to the back of the bus—the action that touched off the Montgomery bus boycott of 1955. Later, he was appointed to a state judgeship by Alabama's segregationist governor, George Wallace. Crosland's godfather, also a lawyer, wrote the speech that Wallace delivered when he became governor, after a campaign in which he ran as a dedicated racist.

In Alabama in general, and Montgomery in particular, the white community's thoughts never strayed far from the time, a century before, when the state had led the South in rebelling against federal authority. On the floor of the state capitol building in Montgomery, there is a star engraved on the spot where, in 1861, Jefferson Davis was sworn in as president of the Confederate States of America. In his inaugural address, Davis proclaimed that slavery was "necessary to self-preservation." When he was a little boy, David Crosland's grandmother and an uncle took him to the capitol, and he stood on that star. He was full of awe and very aware of the history that meant so much to Alabamans.

As a young man, David Crosland had a job selling insurance in Birmingham. The Movement was heating up things in Alabama at the time—there was the Montgomery boycott, and then the Freedom Ride, and race relations were always hot in Birmingham. In the building where Crosland worked, there was a black man who ran the elevators at night. The young white insurance salesman started asking the black man about his thoughts on what was happening.

"It was the first time I'd really talked to somebody who was black *as a peer*, as opposed to somebody who worked for me or my family," said Crosland later. It was amazing, hearing the black man's recollections of growing up in Alabama and contrasting them with Crosland's own feelings. There was also a sense of danger in these meetings. Crosland knew that if anybody found out about their conversations, the elevator operator would be fired, and Crosland might get into serious trouble, too. More than any other place in America, Birmingham tried to make it impossible for whites and blacks to communicate with one another.

Partly because of those conversations, Crosland became

convinced that the system needed changing. He might be able to improve the situation, he thought, if he worked through the legal system. He entered law school. He also lost a few of his white friends by writing letters to the editor of an Alabama newspaper, questioning his home state's position on segregation.

By the time he had finished law school, David Crosland realized that he could not practice law in Alabama in the traditional way—that is, by going along with the segregated system. Very few white lawyers in Alabama who were outspoken in opposing the system could stay in business there. The only one Crosland knew was Charles Morgan, Jr., a Birmingham attorney who courageously represented people in civil rights cases. Even Morgan eventually moved out of the state, to Atlanta. Crosland applied for a job in the Civil Rights Division of the U.S. Department of Justice.

At that time, the Civil Rights Division was the federal government's most energetic agency in combatting segregation. Justice Department lawyers who worked for the division were the cream of the crop. They collected basic information on state-sponsored segregation—the numbers of black children in all-black schools, the discrimination in voter registration and interstate travel. Then, if their superiors in Washington agreed, they brought lawsuits in federal courts to show that the Constitution had been violated and to assure those rights to black Southerners. These Justice Department lawyers, as they were known, were widely respected by members of the civil rights movement. As you might suspect, they were widely despised by segregationists. The most highly respected—and despised—of them was their director, a quiet and brave lawyer named John Doar. (This was the same man Charles Jones had met in McComb, Mississippi.)

When he applied for the Civil Rights Division job, Crosland had asked two federal judges in Alabama to write letters of recommendation. Both men, Judges Frank Johnson and Richard Rives, had ruled frequently in favor of Movement causes, and they were so disliked by racists that they often received threatening mail. The judges were happy to write recommendations, and they sent copies to David Crosland at his family home, where he was staying at the time. His father, who was David Crosland, Sr., the man who had prosecuted Rosa Parks, saw the letters, assumed they were addressed to him, and opened and read them. He was appalled; these two liberal federal judges were saying nice things about his son! What was worse, his son wanted to go to work for the Civil Rights Division!

"He thought it was the worst thing that could have happened to him," said Crosland later. "He cried when he read it. He said he really couldn't face his friends." But the younger Crosland said he was going to seek the job anyway. Relations between father and son were strained after that.

Crosland got the job, and before long he was working on Justice Department matters in Mississippi. He was one of those who participated in the prosecution of defendants in the 1964 murders of three young civil rights workers in Neshoba County, Mississippi. Later, after the passage of the Voting Rights Act, he worked on efforts to enforce the new law in the place where it was most needed—Mississippi. Toward the end of the sixties, he moved north, to Detroit and Cleveland, to collect information on civil rights violations there.

David Crosland's father never became comfortable with the idea that his son was working for the division of the U.S. Justice Department that was trying to bring desegregation to the South. After Crosland took the job, his father would tell friends who asked about him that his son worked for "the Justice Department." He wouldn't say "the Civil Rights Division."

It was a little different with Crosland's godfather, the man who had written George Wallace's inaugural speech. Crosland and his wife were back in Montgomery for the Christmas holidays after he joined the division, and they met his godfather at a party. "I understand you're in Washington," he said. "What are you doing there?"

"Well," replied Crosland, "I'm in the Justice Department." He really didn't want to start an argument with his godfather, particularly on this festive occasion.

"What division?" asked his godfather.

"Civil Rights Division," said Crosland. He wondered if his godfather might become so angered that he would hit him.

"Good," said his godfather. "John Doar's a good lawyer. Stick with him as much as possible. You'll learn a lot."

Val Coleman

In its early years, the civil rights movement was a movement almost exclusively of the American South. Most of the organizations that took part in it were based in the South, and most of the people who marched, protested, and boycotted were Southerners. That should not be surprising. It was the Southern states that had the laws and customs requiring segregation, as well as the elected pol-iticians who promised endless separation. The rest of the nation, by and large, had laws declaring that segregation and official discrimination were illegal. Politicians in the North, Midwest, and West were careful not to anger black people, either because of their personal convictions or because they knew that angry black voters could remove them from office.

By the mid-sixties, however, there was a great awakening in America to the realization that segregation was not just something that went on in Alabama and Mississippi and South Carolina. Blacks and whites in New York, Chicago, and Los Angeles saw that, no matter what the law books said, they lived unequal and largely separate lives. There was discrimination in housing, in education, and partic-ularly in employment. In the North, being "poor" all too often meant being black and being shut out of the same kinds of jobs that were open to white people.

The Congress of Racial Equality, the group that orga-nized the Freedom Ride of 1961, worked in both North and South to challenge segregation and its effects. CORE was born in Chicago, and it had always had a Northern accent. In many ways, CORE was the communications connection between the Movement and the North. And Val Coleman, a young man whose experience was in the movie business, was one of the important links in that connection.

It was in 1959 that Coleman got involved with what soon would be called the Movement. He was working for United Artists, the motion picture outfit, in New York City. His job was getting publicity for the company's movies. But he was rapidly losing interest in his work. One day he called up his sister, a physician, and asked her for advice. She suggested that he get in touch with CORE. She had helped to form some of the group's local chapters back when the organization was started. Val called CORE, which needed people who were skilled at getting its message before the public.

After the Greensboro sit-ins began in 1960, CORE decided to organize sympathy demonstrations in Northern cities. The object, as was seen in chapter 4, was to call attention to the fact that store chains that might not discriminate in New York or Boston or New Haven nevertheless had outlets in Southern cities that *did* discriminate. This was the case with Woolworth's, the variety store that was the target of the first Greensboro demonstration and many protests after that. Woolworth's had stores in many Southern cities, and the lunch counters in most of them were segregated, either by state law or by local custom.

Some newspaper readers and television viewers may have thought that CORE's Northern demonstrations were carefully planned occurrences. But that was not necessarily the case. Events in the Movement happened quickly, and there was not a great deal of time for planning. Those thorough and detailed workshops held by the Nashville students were a luxury that the day-to-day Movement could rarely afford. Besides, everybody was new at the business of running a civil rights movement. A lot of what took place got done by the playing-it-by-ear method.

Coleman and others at CORE quickly recognized the importance of the Southern sit-ins, and they knew that they had to hold sympathy demonstrations in the North—particularly in New York City—as soon as possible. Woolworth's was an obvious target. But the activists didn't even know where all the Woolworth stores were.

"We rode around in a car, looking for them," says Coleman now. "We got a copy of the phone book, the Yellow Pages, and we figured out where all the Woolworths were."

In 1961 CORE's technique with the Freedom Ride was similar. Once the organization decided to undertake the ride, Coleman and others dug out a road map of the South and used a red grease pencil—the kind that is used by publicists and editors to mark photographs without damaging them—and laid out the route.

Much of Coleman's job consisted of dealing with the press. Like all other representatives for organizations who are called spokesmen or press officers, his mission was to get his group's story out to as many people as possible. But (and this was a big "but") he had to be careful not to mislead the press. A press spokesman who got a reputation for too much exaggeration or out-and-out lying on one day would have trouble being believed at all the next time he or she tried to interest a reporter or editor in a story idea. Val Coleman was one of those who walked the delicate line gracefully. Reporters knew they could always trust him.

One of Coleman's big jobs was getting the press to understand that James Farmer, CORE's leader, was an important person—which he was. The press, which likes things as simple as possible, acted most of the time as if it thought the Movement had only one leader, the Reverend Dr. Martin Luther King, Jr. One day in 1965, Coleman suggested that Farmer release a statement to the press on a civil rights issue that was then a hot one in New York: police brutality against members of minority groups. When he picked up one of New York's afternoon newspapers later that day, Coleman was delighted to see his boss's name in big type on the front page. It said "Farmer

137

Says No to Cops," or something similar. "It didn't say *Jim* Farmer or *James* Farmer," recalled Coleman. "It just said *Farmer*. And that was the peak." Coleman knew that CORE and its director had now become household words.

Val Coleman didn't hesitate to straighten out the press when he found it in error. During the Freedom Ride, a famous television broadcaster, whom he identified as David Brinkley, referred to the participants as "the so-called freedom riders." Coleman didn't like that; these people had their heads split open because they were peacefully riding a bus, and a broadcaster seemed to doubt their "so-called" sincerity. He went to a phone and called the network and demanded to talk with Brinkley. He then proceeded to chew out the broadcaster. Later on, says Coleman, he got to know Brinkley, who apologized, and the two became friendly.

Later in the Movement years, the leadership of CORE (as well as that of the Student Nonviolent Coordinating Committee) changed. White people were no longer welcome in the organizations that had once sung "Black and white together." CORE, which had used a lapel button showing white and black hands clasped in friendship, now decided that it should be a totally black-run group. One by one, whites left the organization. Val Coleman was the last to go.

Was he bitter? Perhaps a little. He was saddened, of course. But he was also grateful for the experience of being part of the Movement. It was, he says, an "epiphany"—a term, which originated in the Greek, that means an event that suddenly and clearly reveals the true meaning of something. It was, says Coleman, "a lighted area of time," like a candle that drives out the darkness around it.

"And I got a lot more than I gave," he said. "The Movement made me part of the stream of history. It was the most exciting, unbelievable time of my life."

Constance Curry

Many of the whites who were part of the civil rights movement saw that they could be most useful if they served as links between the white and black communities in the South. One of the problems that people always mentioned in discussions of race relations in those days was the "lack of communications" between the races.

In the South, black people and white people worked and lived quite closely together—in fact, a lot of their housing was less segregated than in the cities of the North—but they did a terrible job of communicating with one another. Whites had little understanding of what Negroes felt or how their lives were lived, and blacks knew little of what went on in whites' minds. Several organizations, particularly those connected with religious groups, tried to set up useful communications in the fifties and sixties. They hoped that once people started talking together, their fears and hatreds would decline.

Constance Curry, who's known as Connie to her friends, was one of those who tried to build communications. She used the color of her skin, which was white, to get her in the front doors of other white people's homes in Georgia and Mississippi to talk with them about race relations and to get them thinking about communicating.

Connie was born in New Jersey. Her family moved to North Carolina when she was in the second grade. She grew up in Greensboro. White Southerners who were active in the civil rights movement are frequently asked how they got "the way you are," as if it was somehow unusual for a white person to oppose segregation. (In fact, *many* white Southerners were angered and saddened by the system they saw around them. Only a few, however, had the courage to speak out and do something about it.) When Curry is asked how she got the way she was, she replies that she doesn't have the slightest idea. She does remember an incident in her childhood, though, that demonstrated that she opposed racism from an early age.

She was in the third grade in Greensboro. It was, of course, an all-white school. Connie was going through the lunch line at the cafeteria. The class bully, a big, tall boy, said something nasty to one of the black women who was serving the food. "I think the word *nigger* was in it," says Curry. "I don't know what possessed me to say this, but I turned to him and said, 'You should not say that. That woman is just as good as your mother.'

"And on the playground later on, he knocked me down. I had my new raincoat on—a new brown-and-yellow raincoat. And mud spattered on the yellow lining and on my collar." She says she'll never forget the incident.

Curry went to college at Agnes Scott in Decatur, Georgia, a town adjacent to Atlanta. She became active in student government, and that involvement led to her participation in the National Student Association (NSA), an organization that concerned itself with student issues and kept campus leaders from around the country in touch with one another. The NSA held conventions each year, and during her college years Curry attended them. She made plenty of friends at these meetings, and some of them were black.

Black and White Together

In 1954, the year of the *Brown* decision, Curry went to a student meeting in Atlanta. The gathering was held at a Young Men's Christian Association office. Both blacks and whites attended. (Atlanta didn't have the same harsh requirements for racial separation in nonpublic places as did Birmingham.) But when lunch time came, the black delegates, one of whom was a friend Curry had made at an NSA convention, went to a restaurant in the black business district, and the white delegates went to a white restaurant. Curry was saddened and angry. "We couldn't eat together," she remembers. "It was the law. And that's when I realized that this was going to make a difference in my life. It hadn't made an impact on me personally until then."

After Agnes Scott, Curry won a Fulbright Scholarship to study in France, and then she received a scholarship to Columbia University in New York. In 1957, she went back to the South and took a job as a "campus traveller" promoting the work of the United Nations. She went from college to college in the South, trying to establish local groups to support the international organization. Many of the schools were all black, and Curry became accustomed to being the only white face on a campus. Then the National Student Association asked her to do some travelling for *it*—to hold interracial meetings on Southern campuses where students could discuss a variety of issues, not just racial ones. The idea, again, was to promote communications, to get black and white students comfortable with talking together and exchanging ideas.

She was in Greensboro on February 1, 1960, when the sit-ins started. "And that changed everything," she says. She went to the demonstrators' Easter meeting in Raleigh.

Although she was only a couple of years older than the students, she was named an adult advisor to the newly formed Student Nonviolent Coordinating Committee, along with the legendary Ella Baker. The students valued Constance Curry for many reasons, but one of the practical ones was that she let them use her office mimeograph machine.

In 1964, Curry joined the American Friends Service Committee, which is affiliated with the leading American Quaker organization, as its Southern field representative. One of her first assignments was to head for Jackson, Mississippi, with Jean Fairfax, a member of the Service Committee staff who was black. Three Mississippi counties were under federal court orders to desegregate their schools, and the idea was that Curry would work in the white community and Jean Fairfax would work in the black community. Their object was to help Mississippians prepare for the change that was coming and to try to help make that change peaceful. Curry wanted to organize meetings at which better-educated whites, predominantly women, could discuss the issues and work out problems on their own *before* the tense days of desegregation started. The outcome would be an organization of whites that would be called Mississippians for Public Education.

"It was probably one of the harder summers of my life," said Curry. Her best friends, black and white, were across town, working in the offices of civil rights organizations, but she couldn't visit with them because that would blow her cover and reveal her real role. The plan called for her to be introduced as a college friend of one of the local white women—as someone who had witnessed school desegregation in another part of the South and who might be able to help with the situation in Mississippi. She was "visiting" Jackson and was definitely *not* introduced as an "outsider" from the American Friends Service Committee who was trying to bring about desegregation.

The plan almost went awry. At one of the meetings, which was held at the home of a Jackson woman, Curry suddenly realized that among the guests was a woman who knew her true identity. "So I had to get into the closet," she said. She literally hid in the closet during the entire meeting.

There were other times when the danger seemed a lot more serious. When Curry returned to Atlanta after one trip, she discovered that her car had "K.K.K." (for Ku Klux Klan) painted all over it. And after she left Mississippi, she and a coworker, Winifred Green, went to Houston County, in south Georgia, to help local people prepare for school desegregation there. This time they were working with a predominantly black group.

At the end of one day, as the sun was getting low in the west, the police happened by and stopped the women's car. They hauled Curry and Green to jail. As usual, there were no specific charges against the women.

Civil rights workers knew that their lives were in danger much of the time, but they were in particular danger after dark. That was when unidentified people fired guns into homes, when churches that had been used for Movement activities were burned down, and when prisoners mysteriously "disappeared" from their jail cells. Connie Curry and Winifred Green were especially glad, then, to look out the window of the police station and see the black people with whom they had been working all driving up to find out what was going on. The nervous police released the two young women immediately. "Someone in the black community had seen us getting picked up," said Curry. "They told the people we were working with, and they got a big group of people and came down. I don't know what happened; all I know is that they let us out. I was really happy. And I was scared. I was really scared."

But she never stopped working for the Movement.

TWELVE

The Captain of the Picket Signs: Robert Mants

There was no shortage of young freedom fighters when the Movement came to Atlanta. For years, Georgia's biggest city had been a center of education for black Southerners. Its collection of colleges and the university, which together were called the Atlanta University Center, had been furnishing leadership to the region and the nation for many years. It was natural that when the sit-ins began in Atlanta, it was students from the University Center who planned them and carried them out. They called their organization the Committee on Appeal for Human Rights.

It was also natural that Bob Mants, an eleventh-grader who lived one block from the committee's headquarters, should want to take part in the protests. "I saw these young students marching by my house," he said years afterward. "My curiosity led me to stick my nose into other people's business. I wondered what was happening. So I went up there"—up the steps to the committee office.

When the demonstrations took place in Atlanta, they

usually began with gatherings at the University Center. There the demonstrators would decide on their targets for the day. Then the students would walk in a long line through the streets of the Negro community, across a bridge that spanned the city's rail yards, and into downtown Atlanta, where they would sit in at variety stores and department stores that refused to give them equal treatment. Sometimes they would picket the businesses, marching back and forth outside with signs that explained why they were protesting. Sometimes they would both picket and sit in.

Bob started hanging around the committee's office in his spare time. He admired the students who were organizing the demonstrations and who were all several years older than he was. Bob gently suggested that he'd like to march downtown with them and take part in their protests.

"They did not want me to go downtown," he explained later, "because I would be arrested, and I would be by myself. I was the youngest, and I wouldn't go to the same jail" as the other protestors. Rather, he would be sent to a home for juvenile suspects. The students didn't want that to happen.

"So they made me captain of the picket signs. They had these very well-constructed picket signs that could withstand the weather, and they put me in charge of them." He pointed out that, although he was a "captain," he was an officer with no soldiers. Captain Mants made sure the signs were clean and stacked properly at the end of the day so they could be used again for the next demonstration. When the next time came, Bob handed out the signs to the demonstrators as they started downtown.

After a while, Bob got additional duties. "They raised

my status in the Movement to the level of custodial services," he once told a group of former activists. The "custodial services" consisted of cleaning the committee office. Bob was paid three dollars a week for this.

Bob branched out a bit. The students held dances, called Freedom Hops, as fund-raising events, and Bob Mants painted the signs. He helped with office work—wrote press releases, answered the phone. He also sneaked away from time to time and took part in demonstrations. He never ended up in the hands of the police, however.

Many of those who had formed the Committee on Appeal for Human Rights went on to become affiliated with the Student Nonviolent Coordinating Committee. There was a lot of talk then about nonviolence and the "beloved community," and Bob Mants paid attention to what he heard.

For a Southern black person, he explained later, nonviolence was not a strange philosophy at all. "Those of us who were brought up in the Southern way of life understood nonviolence," he said. "We tried to incorporate it as a way of life. For most of us, it was based on the experience of our parents. We knew that it was just not practical to begin talking about violence. My mother told me that in no uncertain terms."

Mants's mother reminded him that she had been brought up in a time when the segregationists and racists routinely used lynching and murder to keep black people down. Any efforts by blacks to use violence of their own would surely result in greater violence from those who opposed them. The young man's conversations with his parents also reminded him that they had done the best

they could, in their time, to beat down the beast of segregation and that soon his own day would come. They told
him, he said, that "when the opportunity presents itself,
we'll each have to move in his own turn. And we will have
to do what our parents could not do in their own
lifetimes."

Bob Mants joined the Movement full-time when he
moved with SNCC to its southwest Georgia project, which
concentrated on registering voters. The headquarters for
that project was in Albany, Georgia. The segregated system was so strong in southwest Georgia that before the
organizers could concentrate on voting, they had to deal
first with the fear that ran through almost every black
person's life.

After a while, Mants returned to Atlanta to go to
school. "I wanted to go to medical school, make a lot of
money, and live happily ever after," he said. But the Movement called him again, and he found himself in south
Alabama, helping to overcome fear and register voters in
Selma and surrounding counties. The center of activity—
and also the center of danger—was Lowndes County. As
was the case in southwest Georgia, the campaign was not
just to register voters. Bob Mants and the others tried to
start a cooperative, a club where local people could pool
their money to buy things like seed and food. It would be
like buying from a store, except that the members were
also the owners, and they used the profits to lower their
prices. The activists started a Freedom School and a community library, and they organized quilting clubs.

Lowndes County was every bit as dangerous as any place
in Mississippi, as Mants and the others soon learned.
Nighttime shootings were almost common. In August

1965, when a group of organizers was being released from the county jail, a white man shot and killed one of the group and wounded another. The dead man was Jonathan Daniels, a white student from New Hampshire who was studying for the Episcopal ministry. The wounded man was a Catholic priest from Chicago. An all-white jury released the man who had been accused of the shootings.

Instead of frightening the Movement into pulling out of Lowndes County, the terrorism made organizers work all the harder. And more black people in the county saw that political power would help bring peace and dignity into their lives. By 1966, there were more blacks registered to vote in the county than whites. Eight years before, there had been no Negroes registered at all. The shootings also made a lot of organizers revise their thinking about turning the other cheek if they were attacked. Some of them, including Bob Mants, got guns and planned to use them if it became necessary. After Jonathan Daniels was killed, Mants said, "My mother bought me a gun. A thirty-eight special." But he never had to use it.

In fact, Bob Mants got a lot more firepower out of the ballot box. The high-schooler from Atlanta who used to be captain of the picket signs was elected in 1985 to a four-year term on the Lowndes County board of commissioners, which is the decision-making and lawmaking body for the entire county.

When black people in Lowndes County and elsewhere in the South gained the political power that had been denied them for so long, the Movement won a major victory. But the victory also helped to uncover a major realization: that economic equality was still a long way off;

that desegregation does not necessarily mean integration. Black people in south Alabama could elect whomever they chose to run their local governments, but it still would be a while before the differences of race, particularly those that had to do with economic power, would cease to be of importance. Bob Mants thinks that if he had had a magic wand, he would have made the outcome a little different:

"I would have wanted to see a situation in which black people could merge politically, socially, economically, educationally, and all kinds of ways, in a situation in which they could be respected by other people as human beings. So that it wouldn't be a matter of 'black' and 'white,' but a situation in which people could become fully emancipated 'human beings.' If there's anything that would be my ideal, then that's what it would have been."

THIRTEEN

Transcending Your Heritage: Robert Zellner

One of the great things the Movement accomplished was that it enabled people to go beyond what might have been expected of them, or even what they expected of themselves. Young black people whose great-grandparents had lived under slavery and whose grandparents and parents had been forced to live under segregation might be expected to be so empty of hope that they would have little energy to fight racism. Yet these descendants of slaves not only took on segregation, but they also whipped it.

One way of explaining what they did is to say that they *transcended themselves*. "Transcend" means to go beyond the ordinary limits. When you transcend yourself, you demonstrate abilities that no one knew you had. When you transcend your heritage, you go beyond any expectations that might have been based on your ancestry, or your family's income level, or the part of the country you're from. You beat the odds, push the envelope, defeat the system. And it's not all that unusual. People do it all the time: Look at the athletes who compete in the Olympic games, or the students from poor or one-parent homes who take top academic honors, or the people who have overcome physical disabilities.

In the Movement years, a lot of people transcended themselves and their heritage. Most of them, of course, were dark-skinned Americans. But many others were whites.

Robert Zellner's father was a Methodist minister and a member of the Ku Klux Klan. So was Bob's grandfather on his father's side. Bob's father kept his Klan robes and sword and other paraphernalia in a trunk at home, and when he went to a Klan meeting, he would take the robe and hood out of the trunk and put it on. He did not see anything unusual about a minister of the church being a member of a terrorist organization. Many white people felt that way; they thought of the Klan not as a terrorist group, but as almost an extension of their religion. They thought the Klan, in helping to keep Negroes "in their place" (as the saying went), was doing the right thing.

Bob's father, along with most country preachers, went from church to church, staying no more than a few years in each place. All his churches were small, and most served poor communities in the small-town or rural Deep South—the western Florida panhandle and southernmost Alabama. Bob was born in 1939 near Brewton, Alabama, one of those communities. He had four brothers. Because the family moved frequently, the boys had to go through the process of gaining acceptance in each new community. Usually, this meant that they had to be handy with their fists. Bob Zellner was not brought up with a philosophy of nonviolence.

He *was* brought up in a family that prized independent, questioning thinking, however. Before Bob was born, his father had a chance to go to Europe with a church group that hoped to protect Jews from being persecuted by Adolf Hitler, who was rising to power in Germany. When the Reverend Zellner left on the trip, says Zellner, he was a committed, dedicated klansman. When he returned, he was a changed man.

What happened was this: The Reverend Zellner had been in Russia for several months, travelling by horse sled in weather that was uniformly bitterly cold. He was quite homesick. And then the little group he was with happened upon another group of Americans. They were a band of gospel singers who also wanted to rescue some people from the menace of Hitler. And they were black.

In the years to come, the Reverend Zellner told the story to his family many times. "He said he was so happy to hear somebody who spoke English," said Zellner not long ago. "And these gospel singers not only spoke English, but *Southern* English. He said it made him homesick, and he was so happy to see them." The two groups travelled together for a few weeks. "They ate together and really lived together, and it was the first time he had been in such close touch with black people. And he kept forgetting that they were black.

"Finally," said Zellner, "he came to the conclusion that he might as well just forget that they were black. So he did, and it was the first time he really had a chance to relate to black people as real people. And he said it just ruined him as a klansman."

When Bob's father returned home, he quit the Klan. What's more, he became committed to integration, and he courageously preached to his all-white, Deep South congregations that *they* should feel that way, too. Eventually he discarded the Klan equipment that had been in the trunk. Bob's mother ripped up the Klan robes and made shirts for the boys out of them.

Bob may have been exposed to antisegregationist thinking at home, but that was not the case in the rest of society. When he was thirteen years old, he worked in a little country store. He had an experience similar to that of Charles Jones and June Johnson, only in reverse. When he addressed two older Negro customers as "Sir" and "Ma'am," the store owner chewed him out and explained "the rule" to him. This confused Bob, who knew that *another* rule was that you should be respectful to your elders.

Bob Zellner soon found that his ideas about what was right were at odds with those of a lot of other people. In 1956, when he was in high school, he spoke out in favor of the right of a young woman named Autherine Lucy to enter the University of Alabama. The Supreme Court had ordered the school to admit Lucy. She did enter, in the midst of considerable violence by white students and outsiders, but the school administration and students made life miserable for her. Finally she was expelled for speaking out about her unfair treatment.

Zellner found that *his* speaking out caused trouble, too. His remarks frightened many of his fellow students, he said. "People would immediately get scared and look around and say, 'Don't let anybody hear you say that!' And I'd say, 'Well, *you* heard me say it,' and they'd say, 'Yeah, but I know you and I know you're crazy, and I'm not going to pay any attention to what you're saying. But other people will hurt you.'

"And I kept trying to get to the bottom of it. I'd say, 'Well, who *are* these people? I want to meet them.' And nobody would ever tell me who *they* were."

What was behind all these admonitions, Zellner discovered, was fear. The fellow students who looked over their shoulders, he said, "were reacting more from fear than anything else. They weren't thinking about it, they weren't letting themselves feel anything about it; they were just plain scared."

Zellner knew that he could not let that kind of fear get control of him. "I was totally impatient with anybody who would do something based on fear," he said. "I guess I had such a strong founding in the church. My favorite stories were the Christian martyrs, and *they* weren't scared of anything."

After high school, Zellner attended Huntington College in Montgomery, a church-supported school. There, too, he saw people whose actions on racial matters were controlled by fear. A popular teacher at the college was arrested because the police saw him driving one evening with a young black man in his car. The teacher had been at a cocktail party, and the host had asked if he would give the young man, who had been a waiter at the party, a ride home. The police tried to give the impression that the teacher and the young man had a homosexual relationship. After the arrest, college officials banished him from the campus; they even cut his photograph out of the school yearbook. The teacher left town. He was "absolutely, utterly destroyed" by the school and the police, said Zellner.

Zellner and some other students went to the college president to voice their objection. The president freely acknowledged that he knew the police were wrong and that it was equally wrong for the college to knuckle under. But, he said, "You don't understand what we're up against." Again, fear had taken over.

When the sit-ins started in 1960, says Zellner, "It was like a lot of fresh air." And when the Freedom Ride took place in the following year, Zellner got some fellow students together and went down to the Montgomery bus station to serve as observers—to record what happened. They were shocked to find a terrible mob scene. It was at a hospital afterward that Zellner met some of the heroes of that ride, who were also victims of the riot. They were people he would soon get to know very closely.

In the summer of 1961, the Student Nonviolent Coordinating Committee needed a staff member who could travel to the campuses of white colleges, organizing young people who were sympathetic to the Movement. Obviously, it was a job for a white person. Bob Zellner got it, and in September 1961, he showed up at the SNCC office in Atlanta to start work.

The office, he remembers, was "just a little room about the size of a big closet." A young black man sat behind a desk. When Zellner introduced himself, the man stood up, handed him a briefcase, and said, "Don't let this out of your sight."

Zellner recalled, "He got up, and he put on his hat and everything, and he said, 'Well, I've got to be going now.' I said, 'When are you coming back?' He said, 'I'm not coming back.' "

Zellner thought he meant he wouldn't be back that day. " 'When will you be back tomorrow?' " he asked. "He said, 'I'm not coming back tomorrow, either. It's time for me to go back to school.' "

And with that, Bob Zellner became the office manager of SNCC. His chief job was to take telephone messages from people wanting to reach the organization's field secretaries, many of whom were in Mississippi. It was a week before James Forman, SNCC's executive secretary, showed up and welcomed Zellner as SNCC's first white field secretary.

A few days after that, Zellner was in McComb, Mississippi, attending a meeting with many of the other SNCC organizers, when a group of local high school students started a protest march to the courthouse. One by one, the SNCC staffers left their meeting to join the march. Frantic thoughts raced through Zellner's mind. He explained it all later:

"I said to myself, 'Who's going to go?' And I said to myself, 'Of course, *I* can't go. I've got to go to white Southern campuses. I don't want to get arrested; because then how can I ever get on campus?' And I said, 'Plus, my parents are going to get in trouble. My mother is a school teacher; she'll lose her job. My father won't be able to have a church anymore. Plus the fact that I'm going to be the only white person, and there might be more violence. And so I'm glad that I know that I can't go.'

"Nobody said anything, like, 'You should go,' or 'You shouldn't go.' But there was that feeling that came over me. Somebody said, 'Well, it's getting dark; if we're going to go, we've got to go.' So downstairs they went. And all of a sudden I said to myself, 'What are you doing? Here are these kids in Mississippi. They are going to go and *march*. The first march ever like that in Mississippi. . . . What's going to happen to *them*? What's going to happen to *their* parents?' And everything paled into insignificance.

"And I said, 'If I'm going to be a SNCCer, I've got to

be a SNCCer.' I just fell in line, and away we went. I don't think I ever would have been a SNCCer if I hadn't done that. Because what SNCC was, was: When it was time to do it, you had to do it."

The marchers were met by klansmen and others who beat them brutally with clubs, blackjacks, and bricks. Zellner was caught in the middle of it all, and he came in for special attention because he was white. Black SNCC staffers tried to protect him by shielding him with their bodies, but the crowd separated Zellner from them and proceeded to almost kill him. A member of the mob tried to gouge Zellner's eyes out and even succeeded in pulling one of his eyeballs out of its socket for an agonizing moment. Miraculously, there was no permanent damage. After the violence had gone on for several minutes, Zellner was taken into the police chief's office—which seemed safer than being outside, even though the police had done nothing to stop the mob.

Then the police chief handed Zellner back over to the mob, which threw him into a car and headed off into the countryside. They stopped in a cow pasture and took Zellner out. A man reached into his truck and produced a rope with a hangman's knot in it.

Bob Zellner was terrified, but he refused to show fear. Instead, he yelled at the group, looking each of them straight in the eye and calling them cowards. "This made them even madder," he later wrote, "but I was certain they were going to kill me anyway, and for some reason, I wanted them to think of me later as not being afraid."

There was some chatter on the citizens band radios in the mob's trucks. Then, for a reason that Zellner does not know, the men changed their minds. They put away the rope and threw him back into a truck. They drove to the county seat and turned him over to the jailer. "I remember feeling a great surge of relief when I heard the heavy door clang shut and the lock snap into place," wrote Zellner later. "I was in jail for the first time in my life, but I felt much safer than being out on the street."

Zellner's wounds healed quickly. His bruises went away and his sore eye returned to normal. He survived the day, and so did his rule about coping with fear. Using fear to try to make someone do what you want, he always felt, is "not a legitimate basis for something to be done." If the person who is being terrorized does not give in to the terror, he or she has defeated the oppressor.

"And the other point," he says, "is that it just isn't *right* to give in to fear. If you compromise your principles because you're afraid something is going to happen to you, then that kills your soul. It makes you a smaller person. It makes you less of a human being. My feeling was always that that's a sacred part of your own self that you have to protect. You can't give that to anybody, even on pain of death."

It also helps, say Zellner and many others from the Movement, if you are part of a group and your goal is to improve conditions for the entire group. "I think it's much easier to have great courage if you're doing something for the common good, rather than strictly for yourself," he said. "Courage, to me, is the ability to do something in spite of, or in the presence of, a very strong fear."

Bob Zellner had joined SNCC, it will be remembered, to help communicate the Movement's message to the world of the white Southern college student. He was going to travel to the campuses of white colleges, explaining what SNCC was doing and, he hoped, making friends for the Movement. He also hoped to dispel any incorrect beliefs the white students might have, not only about the Movement but also about blacks in general. Although the white and black races lived side by side in the South and saw each other every day and in many cases even worked together, whites were amazingly ignorant about the lives of black people. Many whites thought blacks "smelled different," and there was endless talk about the kinkiness of "black hair." Many whites were convinced that you could tell if someone was a Negro by looking at his or her fingernails. If there were no crescent-shaped sections at the base of the nails, then the person was certainly black.

What happened in McComb kept Zellner from starting the campus traveller job, as did the other campaigns that kept popping up—Albany, Baton Rouge, and Danville, Virginia. But finally there was a lull in the struggle, and James Forman suggested that Zellner visit a college campus. But it wasn't a white campus at all; Forman asked Zellner to go to Talladega College, a black school in central Alabama. The students felt it was time for desegregation to take place in businesses in the small town of Talladega, and SNCC wanted to instruct them in direct action and nonviolence techniques.

On the day Zellner arrived, most of the students gathered to hear what the celebrated SNCC field secretary had to say. The president of the student body introduced him. Zellner explained SNCC's history, and he said that he would be setting up evening workshops in direct action.

After the meeting and the dinner that followed, Zellner was sitting on a bench on the campus when a young black woman sat down beside him. She said, "You know, Bob, when you were introduced up there, I could have sworn you were white. You're about the whitest of any Negro I have ever seen."

Zellner, who is cabable of sensing the humor in practically any situation, didn't tell the young woman that he *was* white. "I said, 'How'd you know I was black?' She said, 'Well, when you smiled, I saw your dimples. White people don't have dimples.' "

"I didn't do anything to change her mind. It was sort of cruel. We had a long discussion about white people and black people and how it was what was inside you that made you 'black' or 'white.' . . .

"So about three or four days later, after we were into our workshops, the same young woman came up and she fixed me with a steely stare, and she said, 'You *are* white!' "

Someone had told the student that this young man who looked so white really was white. Zellner recalled, "I said, 'Well, does that make a big difference?' And she said, 'You *fooled* me!' "

The student's indignation didn't last long, and soon she realized that Zellner was someone with whom she could talk about the differences and nondifferences between the races. Zellner laughed as he remembered the conversation: "She'd say, 'May I feel your hair?' I'd say, 'Yeah, you can feel my hair.' 'Can I smell your hair?' 'Yeah, you can smell my hair.' She said, 'You know, that does not smell like dog fur!'

"Then she said, 'When it gets wet, does it smell like chicken feathers?' She had all these stereotypes that she had been taught. Everything that you'd ever heard about white people, she had heard. So now she was convinced I was a white person, so she could find out all these things from the source."

Bob Zellner got more than his share of questions from people, both black and white, who wanted to know why he had joined the Movement. Many of them wanted to know why he had "come South to help the black people." He explains it this way:

"First of all, I didn't come South, because I was *already* South." As he had pointed out to the mob in McComb that was threatening to hang him, he was actually from farther South than they were. Brewton was not far from the Gulf of Mexico.

"And I didn't do what I did necessarily to 'help the black people.' If it helped the black people, that was fine. But the way I got involved in the Movement was through fighting for my own rights. *I* was not allowed the right to assemble, or even the right of academic freedom." He remembered the times when the officials of his own high school and college tried to silence him for his controversial views on race relations.

"I had no First Amendment rights, the rights of freedom of speech. And all this was on the altar of racism.

"And so, in order to have my *own* rights as a citizen, I had to fight for the rights of *all* people. So, actually, I was fighting for my own rights. I had as much at stake in it as anybody had."

FOURTEEN

Afraid *Not* to Do It:
Diane Nash

When Diane Nash was growing up in Chicago, her family tried to protect her from the hurts and pains of racism. Many Negro mothers and fathers did that; it is a normal thing for parents to do. No matter how badly they themselves might have been hurt in life—whether from poverty, bad health, racial discrimination, or just plain bad luck—most parents want to insulate their offspring from life's painful moments.

"My family had the attitude that the older generations were the ones who teach the oncoming generation how to be prejudiced," Nash recalled not long ago. "And they didn't want that to happen with me. They sheltered me from racism."

The neighborhood Diane lived in, on the south side of Chicago, was a segregated one. As a result, it was even easier for her to be sheltered. Black people owned many of the businesses that held the neighborhood together and made it a liveable one: a poultry market, a pharmacy, grocery stores. Diane's mother went to downtown Chicago every day to her job as a keypunch operator, and so she was constantly in touch with the real world where some people were bigoted and some weren't. But when she was a little girl, Diane knew and heard little about that real world.

Her mother and father had been divorced when she was very small, so Diane spent a lot of time with her grandparents. "I was the apple of my grandmother's eye," she says. "She used to play little games with me while she would wash my face or dress me. She would tell me how important I was, and how *precious* I was. She'd say I was worth more money than there was in existence. And I'd say, 'Worth more than a hundred? Thousand?' The numbers would go up and up, as high as I knew. 'Worth more than a million?' And each time she'd say, 'Oh, that's not even close. *Much* more than that!'

"You know, I *believed* her when she told me how valuable and precious I was. I really was given a message by my family that as a human being, I was very important, and should be respected."

It was not until Diane Nash went to Nashville that she realized that not everybody shared her grandmother's feelings. After Diane finished high school, she entered Howard University in Washington, D.C. Then, in 1959, she moved to Fisk University, one of the predominantly black schools in Nashville, as a transfer student. It was in Nashville that she met segregation head-on.

She and a young man were attending the Tennessee State Fair, a large, outdoor agricultural and entertainment festival, in the fall of 1959, and she needed to use the rest room. For the first time, she saw the signs: WHITE WOMEN. COLORED WOMEN.

Nash was outraged. She remembered the little games her grandmother would play, and she thought, as she looked at the discriminatory signs, "You're saying that to her granddaughter? You don't know who I *am!*" Her indignation was apparent to everyone around her, including her date, a Southern black who had known discriminatory signs all his life and who became decidedly nervous about Nash's state of mind.

Diane Nash didn't just fume about discrimination. She tried to do something about it. She searched the Fisk campus and the other black colleges for fellow students who shared her anger about the system and who wanted to change it. A student, one of the few whites at the college complex, told her about a group that was holding discussions of nonviolence as a way to challenge racial discrimination. The leader was a young man named James Lawson.

The Nashville group was working its way toward putting its discussions into action (and the action would be a public demonstration) when the Greensboro sit-ins started in February 1960. Quickly, the Nashville group began its own sit-ins. Diane Nash was among the leaders. Soon she was elected chairperson of the Nashville Student Movement, and when students met in Raleigh at Easter weekend in 1960, she went. She became one of the founding members of the Student Nonviolent Coordinating Committee. And when, in 1961, violence in Alabama forced the Congress of Racial Equality to cut short its historic Freedom Ride, it was Diane Nash and other students from black colleges in Nashville who took up the ride.

Many people wanted the students to abandon their plans to keep the ride going. The threat of violence was too great, they said. But Diane Nash argued that the ride must not be allowed to stop. She was, she said at the time, afraid to continue the ride, but she was *more* afraid not to. She explained that statement this way:

"If the signal was given to the opposition that violence could stop us, then I knew that whenever we tried to do anything in the Movement in the future, we were going to meet with a lot of violence. And we probably would have to get a number of people killed before we could reverse that message." In other words, to back down now would only encourage the segregationists to use even more violence.

Nash, along with many of her fellow students from Nashville, had given a great deal of thought to the meaning of what they were doing. In those workshops that James Lawson conducted, they discussed the meaning and importance of nonviolence. Sometimes the meetings went on until late at night, and then the students gathered again early the next morning before they went off to classes. They rehearsed what they would do if, in the midst of a nonviolent demonstration, a segregationist walked up and started acting violently toward them. They practiced ways to curl their bodies into tight balls, with their hands over their heads, to give themselves maximum protection if they were attacked. Even more important, they practiced *not* responding to violence with violence. They divided up sides and played games, with one group being the nonviolent "demonstrators" and the other being the "segregationists." The "segregationists" would use weapons ranging from foul language to spit to their fists. The "demonstrators" learned how to sit there and take it. The object was to learn nonviolence not just in theory, but also as a way of life.

Diane Nash explained all this in 1988, when she spoke at a meeting at Trinity College in Hartford, Connecticut, that was attended by veterans of SNCC's exciting Movement years. Since some of those in the audience were visitors—college students who hadn't even been born in the sixties—she explained what proponents of nonviolence meant when they talked about wanting to build a "redeemed community":

One of the dictionary definitions of *redeem*, she said, is "to recover, as in a pawned watch; to discharge or fulfill a pledge or a promise; to obtain release or restoration, as from captivity, by paying a ransom."

That was what many of the activists of the sixties wanted, she said: a community that was redeemed (sometimes they also called it a "beloved community"). It was "a community recovered or fulfilled, in terms of a community that could become more of what its potential was . . . a community that gave to its citizens all that it could give and allowed its members to then give back to the community all that it could.

"Our goal was to reconcile; to really heal; and to rehabilitate. To solve problems, rather than to simply gain power over the opposition."

What she was talking about, really, was developing *respect* for those who opposed you. Putting that philosophy into action was difficult, particularly when doing so involved coping with opponents who might not *want* reconciliation, who might not subscribe to or even understand the idea of nonviolence, and who didn't have all that much respect for you.

Diane Nash and the other students from Nashville, with the help of James Lawson, developed a five-step process by which they planned their attacks on segregation. To an outsider, a sit-in at a variety store lunch counter might look like something that was thought up on the spur of the moment by a group of high-spirited college students. But to the students themselves, it was the product of much disciplined planning.

The first step in the process was *investigation*. The students conducted research into the problem at hand. If it was lunch-counter discrimination, they analyzed the layout of the building. They studied the importance of black customers to the store. They considered the possible reactions to a demonstration: Would there be violence? If so, how would the store owner react? If the police were called, how would they behave?

The second step was *education*. The students who had done the investigation explained what they had learned to everyone else who planned to take part in the demonstration.

Third came *negotiation*. In this stage, said Nash, "you approached the opposition, let them know your position, and tried to come to a solution." Sometimes the "opposition" was a store owner; sometimes it was a city's mayor or council members.

The fourth stage was the *demonstration* itself. More than likely, this was the first time that the general public learned of the students' grievance and saw the outcome of all their investigation, education, and negotiation. "The purpose of demonstrations," said Nash, "was to focus the attention of the community on the issue and on the injustice." Usually a sit-in demonstration did exactly that. Of course, if the protestors got what they wanted during their negotiations with the opposition, things never had to get to the demonstration stage.

The last stage was *resistance*, which Nash defined as "where you really withdraw your support from the oppressive system." An important ingredient of nonviolence, as practiced by the civil rights movement, was the fact that black people were declaring their unwillingness to support the system that mistreated them. That's precisely what people did in Montgomery when they decided to stop riding on (and paying for) segregated buses. Resistance could mean a boycott, as in Montgomery, or it could mean refusing to work in the stores or homes of the people who mistreated you.

Diane Nash had a long and successful career in the Movement. She worked both for SNCC and Martin Luther King, Jr.'s Southern Christian Leadership Conference, and she played a major role in focussing the attention of Dr. King—and thus of the nation—on Selma, Alabama, as a symbol of segregation and racism. Early in her Movement career, in 1961, she married a fellow activist, the Reverend James Bevel, who was on the SCLC staff. She became a mother during those years. Her daughter, Sherrilynn, was almost born in prison because Diane Nash was a Movement person. It happened this way:

Nash, who then was twenty-four years old, was in Jackson, Mississippi, in 1962, after the original Freedom Ride. Hundreds of people from all over the country were descending on the South to go on their own freedom rides. Many of these rides ended in Jackson, where the police methodically (and illegally) arrested everyone who arrived at the bus station who looked like a demonstrator. There was a need for teaching the new riders about nonviolence and what to expect in jail, and Diane Nash was doing the instructing. She was also encouraging black Southerners to defy the Mississippi state law by riding at the front of the bus.

Some of those she was training were young people. They fit the state's definition of "minors," or people who were not yet old enough to be considered adults. So the police arrested Nash and charged her with "contributing to the delinquency of minors." (The federal courts had ruled, and would rule again, that riding at the front of a bus, or anywhere else, was a basic American right, so anyone who advocated it could hardly be accused of encouraging the breaking of laws. But Mississippi judges, as usual, saw it the other way. They paid little attention to the federal rulings. In their eyes, anyone who advocated desegregation was advocating something that was illegal.)

Contributing to the delinquency of minors is a serious charge, and Nash knew that if she were convicted, she could get as much as two and one-half years in the state prison. In Mississippi, the state prison was a particularly awful place. It was especially so for anyone who had the reputation of a civil rights activist. Being a Movement person was dangerous enough in Mississippi *outside* of prison, but inside, away from the eyes of the world and the support of fellow organizers, all sorts of terrible things could happen.

Nash was convicted in the local court, to no one's surprise. Then she and her attorney appealed the case to a higher court. The appeal process, by which the decision of a lower court is reviewed by a higher one, was a very important one for the Movement. Activists could be fairly certain that courts at the lower levels—particularly the county and state levels—would rule against them. But they had good reason to believe that, once they got their cases into the higher courts, their convictions would be thrown out. While the Movement could be pretty sure that it would win in the end, it frequently took a long time to get to victory. Sometimes a civil rights case had to go all the way to the Supreme Court of the United States before it was settled in favor of the Movement. Since bond was required while a case was being appealed, a lot of money was tied up by the process.

There was a mix-up in Diane Nash's case. Nash says her attorney told her she did not have to appear in person when the time came for her appeal to be considered. The court thought otherwise. When she didn't appear, the judge ordered her bond revoked—it was several thousand dollars that had been posted by the National Association for the Advancement of Colored People—and he issued a warrant for her arrest. Failing to appear after posting bond was sometimes even more serious than the original crime itself. It looked as if Nash would have to go to prison. And Diane Nash was pregnant.

"I had to make a decision about what I was going to do," she recalled recently. Nash knew she could not sell out the people she had been organizing. She and her husband had been encouraging black Mississippians to take risks in the name of freedom—to break the state law by sitting in the front of the bus, by going down to the courthouse to try to register to vote. "And a number of those people had instantly lost their jobs and the houses that they lived in, because they worked on plantations." Some of the plantation owners, once they heard what their tenants were doing, "just fired them and put them off the plantation.

"And so people had taken some risks." Nash and her husband knew that she could probably avoid prison by just leaving the state. It was unlikely that the authorities in Chicago or some other Northern place would pay much attention to the Mississippi warrant. But if she did that, it would mean leaving behind the Mississippians whom she and her husband had encouraged to take so many risks. These were people who did not have the luxury of fleeing their trouble as easily as Nash could.

"So I basically went into my bedroom for about three days and thought," she said. If she gave herself up to the court, she would probably have her baby in prison, and after its birth, it would probably be taken from her and placed in a foster home. "It would mean not knowing my child until the child was about two years old," she said. "I had to really think it through very carefully. For those three days, that's basically all I did: think and meditate.

"And at the end of that time, I emerged knowing with a great deal of power what I would do. It was really a moment of spirtual strength. . . . There was nothing anyone could do to me. I was thoroughly prepared for all eventualities, and had decided to go through them." Diane Nash was ready to go to prison, and even to have her child there. She told her many friends who gathered around her during this crisis that any black child who was born in Mississippi was already in one kind of prison—the prison of segregation—and that the sort of prison she was headed for was not all that different.

James Bevel and Diane Nash went to the courthouse

on a Friday evening, and she turned herself in to the sheriff. He, along with others in the county government, seemed surprised to see that Nash was pregnant. "I was *very* large," she said. "I was about five months' pregnant. I told the sheriff, 'I understand there's a warrant out for my arrest, and I came to surrender.' "

The sheriff looked at Nash and said, "Well, that's the judge's problem. Come back on Monday morning."

When she showed up in the courtroom, she sat in the front row—a row normally reserved for white people. When a court employee ordered her to move to the back, she refused. The judge took one look at his prisoner—a pregnant young woman who obviously was not going to cooperate with the segregated system—and he forgot all about the two and a half years in prison. He sentenced Nash to ten days in jail for refusing to move to the rear of the courtroom, and he ignored the more serious charge. When Nash asked him about it, he said he had decided not to pursue the charge.

Ten days in jail in Mississippi meant that Diane Nash's daughter would not be born in prison, but it wasn't exactly a fun time. The jail was infested with cockroaches. Nash watched them enough to conclude that, as she put it later, they were "deliberately climbing up over my bed and then dropping down!" She had a few essentials—a toothbrush and change of clothing—and she worked out a schedule for keeping her clothes and herself clean. "I learned to comb my hair with my fingers," she said. "I learned that I could exist on just food and water." Being in jail, she said, "really served the opposite purpose that I'm sure they intended. Because I learned that I was stronger than I ever knew I was."

FIFTEEN

A Whole New World

An entire generation of Americans has grown up in the years since the Movement began. It is time, now, to reflect on what happened during those years of dramatic change: on what the Movement accomplished, on what it didn't accomplish, and on what's next.

Like all examples of far-reaching social change, the civil rights movement never really had an ending point. The events that started it and kept it going simply gave life to a struggle that goes on today. That struggle will continue, in one form or another, as long as there is inequality in the way dark-skinned people are treated. And plenty of inequality remains in most of the areas that the Movement addressed: education, housing, employment and economic opportunity, and justice.

So, in one way of thinking, the Movement just keeps on marching. It would be impossible to neatly add up all its accomplishments and its failures and to say, "This is what the Movement was and what it did." But we can study what happened, and we can sort out what we've learned so far, and we can apply that learning to the conditions we find around us today.

One important lesson the Movement taught us is that when ordinary people get together behind an important goal, they can do extraordinary things. There is a well-worn saying, "The whole is greater than the sum of its parts." That saying applies, as well, to the Southern movement: The total change that was caused by all those people working together was far greater than anything they could have done working individually.

Those individuals who made up the Movement came in all shapes and sizes, all ages, all shades of skin color. Some had a lot of formal education, and some had none. Some had money to spend, and some had to worry about how they were going to pay for their next meal. Some were nice, and some were nasty. Some were beautiful, and some were homely. In other words, they were like people in general. But when they all gathered together into something we learned to call the Movement, they were a disciplined, energetic, powerful force that could not be stopped by all the segregationist laws, politicians, judges, and terrorist night-riders of the South.

The people who made up the Movement, thinks Julian Bond, were "special, but they weren't extraordinary." Bond was a young man in Atlanta during the Movement years, a student at the Atlanta University complex. He was the communications director for the Student Nonviolent Coordinating Committee; later on, he became a Georgia lesiglator. Movement people, he says now, "were no different from their colleagues and classmates. What made them special was their stick-to-itiveness." It was true

175

then, as it is now, that the willingness to stick with a project, to slog away at it, is the best way to turn that dream into a success.

Bond warns young people against thinking that the Movement's accomplishments were easy ones or assuming that the struggle was just a series of protests that immediately produced victories. People who think that, he says, may mistakenly believe that if they want to tackle a big social problem today, all they have to do is put on a demonstration and sit back and wait for results. "It takes a whole lot more than that," he says. "It takes the sort of organizing work that these people did in the sixties—going around to the college dormitories during the sit-ins, handing out leaflets, and then later, when the Movement moved off the campus into the community, the knocking on doors, the walking down the streets, the mass meetings—all building, building, building, slowly until you had a critical mass big enough to do something in the community." (*Critical mass* is a term from the world of science that refers to the amount of accumulated energy that is needed in order to produce a reaction, such as an atomic explosion.)

Producing critical mass in something such as the civil rights movement is like getting a huge rock to roll down a hill. You need to smooth out the dirt in front of the rock first, and perhaps remove the obstacles—smaller rocks and debris. Then you push against the rock, or maybe you use a heavy stick to produce leverage. You might want to ask several of your friends to help with the pushing. It's very difficult at first. It almost seems as if the big rock doesn't want to budge. But then there's a little motion, a stirring. It increases and increases until the rock is finally moving.

After that, it seems almost easy. And finally, it's "Look out below!"

Once a local movement began to move of its own momentum, wonderful things started to happen. Martha Prescod Norman, a young black woman who was a SNCC field secretary in Mississippi and Selma and who now teaches African-American history at Wayne State University in Michigan, witnessed that sort of change from some of the toughest places in the South.

"The important thing," she says, "was that we were making change. We were changing the society. It felt as if you were pushing history. You had your hands up against the society, and you were pushing, and you could feel it move."

Norman also reminds her students today that it's wrong to think that the Movement had to have a single, powerful leader to make it happen. A lot of people assume today that it was just one person, the Reverend Dr. Martin Luther King, Jr., who was responsible for everything that occurred in the Movement. Martha Norman, while acknowledging that Dr. King was a much-appreciated and valuable leader, disagrees. What gave the Movement that power to "push history," she says, was a combination of factors. For one thing, black Americans already had a lot of experience with operating and participating in organizations—churches, community improvement associations, the early boycotts. This created a climate where leadership could flourish. When all that community spirit combined with the students' willingness to fight segregation even at the cost of going to jail, the Movement was truly born. "Once people were willing to go into motion and risk their life and limb," says Norman, "that was the end of the system."

Diane Nash agrees. "I think that freedom is people realizing that they are their own leaders," she says. "It would be more comfortable if it were true that there was someone who had all the answers. But that person doesn't exist. The answer is in each of us."

The Movement also reminded everyone, not just Americans, that the desire for change is universal. It does not apply just to Americans with dark skins who live in the South. While the Movement was going on, it was being watched by people around the globe who had their own needs for freedom and who found in the Movement their key to action. It was because of what happened in the civil rights movement of the sixties that dozens of *other* movements were begun. The Movement, then, freed more than black Southerners; it helped the entire world to become a bit more free.

White college students from the West and North who had participated in Freedom Summer in Mississippi and Louisiana returned to their college campuses in the fall—most notably the University of California at Berkeley—and formed their own movement around the issues of freedom of speech and student rights. The women's movement, which had been in existence in the United States for a long time, suddenly got the burst of energy that it needed to become a major force, thanks to the civil rights movement. People who found themselves placed in many other groups and categories, ranging from adoptees to gay Americans to those who both favor and oppose the right of women to have abortions, got much of their enthusiasm and guidance from the civil rights movement.

And in the formerly Communist countries of Europe and in the People's Republic of China, when citizens announced they had had enough of their repressive governments, they accompanied that announcement by singing "We Shall Overcome."

Another lesson that could be drawn from the Movement is that it helps a great deal to have a strong, supportive family. Many of those who participated in the Movement say that they received the strength to do what they did from mothers, fathers, or grandparents. These were the people who told them, as did Diane Nash's grandmother, that they were "precious," worth much more than a million dollars, or maybe a trillion.

American life has changed a lot in the years since then, and *family* life has changed more than almost anything else. Parents have to work harder to make a living, and so they have less time to spend with their children. Everybody seems in much more of a hurry now. Grandparents may be finishing out their lives in institutions with other older people, rather than in the family home. There are far more one-parent families these days. The television set has been assigned the job of raising children. Illegal drugs have torn some families apart. The community in which young people live is less likely to be a self-sustaining one, with home-owned businesses and residents who are from a variety of income levels and occupations and who serve as models for the young people of the neighborhood. The "community" may not even be a real community at all. It may be little more than a collection of apartments or houses in the center of the city or in the suburbs that you leave when you want to go to the mall.

In short, it's harder these days to find someone who will remind you that you're precious.

But that doesn't mean there aren't adults around—in schools, libraries, churches, community organizations—who want to help younger people appreciate their own value. People who are veterans of the Movement years seem to be especially mindful of the need to pass on their thoughts and experiences to girls and boys.

When those former Movement people are asked how they would translate the lessons of those days to today's conditions, they acknowledge that the translation is not an easy one. The obstacles of yesterday, such as being denied a seat at the lunch counter or in the bus terminal waiting room, they say, seem almost simple when they are compared to today's economic problems of race. How do you provide employment when businesses are shutting down? How do you help the mother of three who receives welfare assistance, and who wants to improve her education and get a job, when there's no money in the social services programs, and political leaders seem not interested in doing very much about the problem?

The veterans also point out that it might be hard to duplicate some of the ingredients of the Movement, that were so important back then, such as those freedom songs that generated so much courage, or the sheer human power that flowed through the hot, sweaty mass meetings (many of the poorest churches have air conditioning now). But that doesn't mean that there aren't ways in which the Movement can be continued, or that there isn't good reason why it *should* be continued.

Nonviolence is just as useful today as it was in 1960.

Diane Nash notes that nonviolence back then "was remarkably effective in the South. We really achieved the goals that we set for ourselves . . . and with relatively few casualties. I think it would be very good if more people would really study that philosophy and that strategy, and apply the principles to the struggles today." Other techniques that Diane Nash and her fellow students used in the sixties are equally valid in coping with the problems of today. The Nashville students' five steps to carrying out a direct action campaign, as described in chapter 14, might be just as useful today in doing something about homelessness, or the destruction of tropical rain forests, or teenage pregnancy. Diane Nash says: "Young people, if they think about it, can come up with real specifics on things that they see in society that need changing. I think the only thing you can do is do the best that you can. Get involved with groups that are trying to do something about these problems."

The most productive years of the Movement were those in which both black and white Americans joined together to battle discrimination. Later on, for a number of reasons, many whites drifted away from the struggle. Some felt they were no longer wanted (or they were told they weren't wanted), and some got interested in other issues, such as trying to end the Vietnam War.

Any continuation of the Movement today, say those who were its heroes, has got to be a joint black-white effort. The issues are just too big to be handled by only one segment of America. Says Leslie McLemore:

"Clearly we went through a stage in our history where black people said, 'We can do it ourselves; we really don't need any more support from the white community.' But the older I get, the more I am convinced that we aren't going to work ourselves out of these dilemmas by just black people attacking these issues themselves. It's going to take a coalition of black people, white people, brown folk, and whatever, in order to deal with these issues effectively." Rebuilding that coalition would be one of the greatest contributions that young people today could possibly make.

And if they make it, they'll be better equipped to tackle one of society's toughest problems: economic inequality. It's the problem that the Movement of the sixties helped to reveal, and that remains unsolved to this day. Les McLemore says:

"The real test now, the next step right now, is how you deal with the economic empowerment of blacks and other minorities. How can you take advantage of the gains made during the Movement? So often, those gains have been translated into political empowerment for black people—the right to run for office, or the right to vote. And so many positions have been captured by black officeholders. But the real crucial test now is, how does one take advantage of the political empowerment and connect that to economic development? And that is the real test. That's the real challenge. And, quite frankly, we have not figured out a way to do that. We have not figured out a way to use the energy from being elected to office to economically improve the conditions of people."

Figuring out that would seem to be a good challenge for young people today.

Robert Zellner uses an old-fashioned word to describe what he thinks would help young people attack the problems of society: "Gumption." It means employing practical common sense to cope with the problems of living. The heroes of the Movement had plenty of that. Says Zellner:

"Prejudice is still with us. Oppression is still with us. There's lots of injustice in the world. And they have to be fought.

"Now, number one, you have to have the gumption to fight it. To get that gumption, you have to be inspired by something." That inspiration could come through an appreciation of what happened in the Movement years.

"And the second thing is, you have to know how to go about fighting it. And to me, one of the most important things for young people is to have integrated experiences. *Integration* is a very unused word now. But integration itself has a positive value. And it's probably more difficult now to have an integrated experience than it was thirty years ago.

"An integrated experience is wonderful, and those of us who were in the Movement know that. I think I was one of the most privileged people in the world to go through the experiences I went through. I wouldn't take *anything* for them. And because we went through those experiences, we are welded together in an extremely special way.

"So you've got to have integrated experiences. The best way to do that is to fight along with someone for something that's important to both of you."

Charles Jones enjoys receiving requests from school groups to visit their classes and explain what it was like back in the days of McComb and Albany and Selma and

Raleigh. He is always struck by the fact that when he is talking about the Movement, he's discussing something that to him is just as real as yesterday—but to the third- and sixth- and seventh-graders he's visiting, it might as well be ancient history.

He deals with this problem by drawing a verbal picture of the system in which he grew up. He asks his listeners to imagine that they attended "a totally segregated school, in a totally segregated community, in a totally segregated public environment," where, no matter "how well they behaved, they were always considered black. And they could be arrested for what they take for granted now," such as drinking from a water fountain or sitting in the front of a bus.

Gradually, says Jones, the students to whom he speaks begin to understand why it was necessary and important for him and the other young people of the Movement to stand up and say, "We are not going to accept this kind of behavior anymore."

And then Jones tells the students about what the Movement people did—the risks they took, the nonviolent battles they fought—and he says to those in his audience who are black:

"This is what your history is. This is what your heritage is. You come from cultures that, prior to most of European history, were performing architectural feats that are still manifested in the Pyramids. You're talking about a culture out of which came a tremendous sense of commitment to the individual and the integrity of the person and respect for each other and the earth.

"And it's your history. And here's another phase of it that I went through, some thirty years ago. You have this opportunity now, as a member of the global community, to understand and make a change, not only in yourself individually, but those around you. And I think it's for *you* to figure out how to do that.

"So I say, 'You have the capacity to do it. We're certainly here to help, but you have the ability to make change, just as we did.' "

Scenes from the Civil Rights Movement

An example of a picket line from the sixties. This one promotes fair employment practices at an Atlanta bakery.

Youthful protestors kneel and pray in front of city hall in Albany, Georgia, in the summer of 1962, at the height of the Albany Movement's antisegregation activities. The police watched the youths for a few minutes, then arrested them. Almost all were black, but some were white—including the tall young man in the center, SNCC worker Bill Hansen. At left, *New York Times* reporter Claude Sitton takes notes.

When the University of Georgia admitted two young blacks from Atlanta to its undergraduate body under a federal court order in the sixties, anti-integrationists tried to make sure that the students, Charlayne Hunter and Hamilton Holmes, knew that they weren't welcome. NEGRO GO HOME says the sign painted on the side of this shed on the highway from Atlanta to Athens. Both students turned out to be good ones: Holmes is a member of the university's board of trustees, and Charlayne Hunter (now Charlayne Hunter-Gault) is a correspondent for public television's "Macneil/Lehrer NewsHour."

The Reverend Dr. Martin Luther King, Jr., and his wife, Coretta, arrive at the Albany city hall on February 27, 1962. Dr. King, along with more than seven hundred other blacks, had been arrested in December 1961 during a "prayer march" in downtown Albany. The demonstrators were charged with "parading without a permit." Now Dr. King is returning for his trial.

One of the most memorable characteristics of the civil rights movement was its singing. Songs, many of them adapted from church anthems and some of them borrowed from the labor movement, held the demonstrators together and nourished their courage. Singing was never better than in the hot summer of 1962 in Albany, Georgia. In the photo a group of young civil rights activists, known as the Freedom Singers, holds forth behind the pulpit of a church. They sang at a mass meeting, one of many called to inform the black community of the Movement's progress. Such meetings often ended in marches downtown—where, in Albany, arrest was almost always certain.

When they held sit-in demonstrations at downtown Atlanta variety and department stores, young black students from the Atlanta University Center would march from the campus down to the viaduct that spanned the city's rail yards and separated a black community from downtown. Here a long line of demonstrators heads for the bridge and the downtown skyline.

When black students began their sit-ins in Atlanta, many merchants responded by closing their facilities. LUNCH DEPARTMENT CLOSED says this sign on the counter at Woolworth's in downtown Atlanta. It was placed there shortly after students from the Atlanta University Center arrived. Two of the students are visible at the end of the counter.

SOME IMPORTANT EVENTS

1619   The first Negroes arrive at Jamestown, Virginia, in the British North American colonies. They are known as indentured servants, rather than slaves, but they are not free people.

1857   The Supreme Court of the United States rules in the *Dred Scott* case that Negroes do not have citizenship.

1862   For a year, most of the slaveholding South has rebelled against the federal government in the Civil War. President Abraham Lincoln delivers the Emancipation Proclamation. He declares that on January 1, 1863, all the slaves who live in states that are rebelling against the national government shall be free.

1866   The Civil War ends. The national government is victorious.

1895   Booker T. Washington, the black educator, delivers a speech at the Atlanta Exposition. He says that education and self-help are the keys to Negro independence, rather than integration with the white society.

1896   The Supreme Court rules that it is legal for the races to be "separate but equal." The case is called *Plessy* v. *Ferguson*. It will form the basis of American race-relations law for the next fifty-eight years.

1905   W. E. B. DuBois, the black scholar and writer, calls a conference of Negro leaders in Niagara Falls, Canada. The Niagara Movement, as it was known, strongly protests injustice and influences black thinking and action for years to come.

1909   Blacks and whites, including members of the Niagara Movement, hold a National Negro Conference in New York City. The resulting organization becomes known as the National Association for the Advancement of Colored People (NAACP).

1942   The Congress of Racial Equality (CORE) is organized in the North. One of its first actions is to hold sit-ins at a Chicago restaurant that discriminates against Negroes.

1953   Blacks in Baton Rouge, Louisiana, angry over segregated seating, organize a boycott of the city's buses.

1954   On May 17, the Supreme Court announces its decision in the case of *Brown* v. *Board of Education*. The rule of "separate but equal," says the court, is dead. Segregation in education is illegal.

1955   Emmett Till, a fourteen-year-old black boy from Chicago, is murdered by whites in Leflore County, Mississippi, because he whistled at a white woman. People around the world are horrified.

       The federal transportation agency, the Interstate Commerce Commission, says segregation on interstate bus transportation is illegal.

In December, the Montgomery, Alabama, bus boycott begins after Rosa Parks is arrested for refusing to give her seat to a white passenger. The boycott ends a year later when the buses are desegregated.

1956 Autherine Lucy, a young black woman, enters the University of Alabama under a federal court order. The school's students resist violently, and before long she is forced out.

1957 The Southern Christian Leadership Conference, an outgrowth of the Montgomery bus boycott, is formed. Many of its members are black clergymen. It is directed by the Reverend Dr. Martin Luther King, Jr.

Congress passes a civil rights act that insures greater rights for Negroes to vote and increases the federal government's commitment to fighting discrimination.

When the schools open in the fall in Little Rock, Arkansas, mobs of white people try to prevent blacks from entering Central High School. President Dwight Eisenhower must send in the army to keep order.

1960 On February 1, a handful of black college students in Greensboro, North Carolina, enter a downtown variety store and ask to be served food at the lunch counter. The store refuses to serve them, and the modern sit-in is born. Within a few months, young black people are using the sit-in technique all over the South.

Shortly after the Greensboro demonstration, young blacks and a few whites form a group that will become known as the Student Nonviolent Coordinating Committee (SNCC). It will be one of the hardest working of the frontline civil rights organizations.

1961   In May, CORE sponsors a Freedom Ride on interstate buses through the South. In Alabama, white mobs destroy a bus and savagely beat the riders. CORE eventually calls a halt to the ride, but other activists carry it on.

1962   Civil rights organizations, with help from foundations, start the Voter Education Project (VEP), an effort to encourage voting in parts of the South where blacks have been discouraged from registering before. Although voting is widely regarded as a basic American right, VEP organizers find that their work is dangerous and difficult.

In September, a young black air force veteran named James Meredith attempts to enter the all-white University of Mississippi to complete his education. He is backed by a federal court order, but the state resists him, and the university administration and state authorities allow a huge mob of students and outsiders to gather. A nightlong riot results, and two persons are killed. Finally, federal marshals and troops must fly in to keep order. Meredith is constantly harassed as a student, but he graduates in 1963.

1963   In January, Harvey Gantt becomes the first black student to enter Clemson, a school of higher education in South Carolina. There is no violence. One reason is that South Carolina officials did not want their state to be classified as "another Mississippi."

In the spring, blacks hold demonstrations in Birmingham, Alabama, the most strictly segregated city in the nation. The authorities respond by turning fire hoses and police dogs on the demonstrators, who include children. Shortly afterward, authorities in Danville, Virginia, meet protestors with equal violence.

In June, Alabama Governor George Wallace steps aside (after saying he wouldn't) and allows two black students to enter the University of Alabama.

Medgar E. Evers, the NAACP leader in Mississippi and that state's most respected civil rights leader, is murdered outside his home in Jackson.

In August, the largest demonstration in the history of the nation is held when more than two hundred thousand people take part in the March on Washington. Many politicians and white media people predict violence, but there is none.

On September 15, a Sunday morning, racists set off dynamite at a Negro church in Birmingham. Four children are killed.

1964   Movement organizations, led by SNCC and CORE, sponsor Mississippi Freedom Summer, an effort to organize black communities and register voters in America's most segregated state. The summer is marked by white violence against Movement people. In one case that attracts international attention, three young workers—one black and two white—disappear in Neshoba County. Their bodies are discovered later, buried in an earthen dam. The tragedy leads President Lyndon B. Johnson to force the Federal Bureau of Investigation (FBI) to get actively involved in civil rights matters. Before, the FBI had worked in opposition to the Movement.

Soon after the Mississippi murders are revealed, President Johnson signs into law the 1964 Civil Rights Act. It is the strongest such law so far. But it does nothing to head off rioting by residents of black communities in New York City and other Northern cities.

In August, the Democratic party holds its presidential nominating convention in Atlantic City, New Jersey. A group of blacks and whites from Mississippi attends and argues that the regular delegation from that state should not take part in the convention because it excludes blacks. The convention suggests a compromise, by which the Mississippi Freedom Democratic party (MFDP), as the integrated group is known, would receive token representation. The MFDP delegates consider this an insult.

1965   In March, blacks and whites try to march from Selma, Alabama, to the state capitol in Montgomery in a protest against the denial of voting rights in much of Alabama. Local police attack the marchers with whips and clubs. The incident attracts national attention, and thousands of sympathizers arrive in Selma from elsewhere in the nation. A second attempt to march is successful.

In August, Congress passes the Voting Rights Act of 1965. It is clear that the Selma violence is largely responsible for passage of the law. Shortly after the act is signed into law, federal officials go to the parts of the South where resistance to blacks' voting is greatest. A tremendous increase in black voter registration results.

1966   With many of their major battles won—particularly the campaign for voting rights—the more activist parts of the Movement, CORE and SNCC, start to change their direction. Both began as interracial groups, but now they tell their white members to leave. The traditional groups, such as the NAACP, remain at work on the Movement's goals. There is much work to be done: Although official discrimination has been outlawed in education, transportation, employment, and voting, a great deal needs to be done to turn those laws into reality.

1968   On April 4, Martin Luther King, Jr., is in Memphis, Tennessee, to campaign for better employment conditions for the city's garbage workers, when he is shot to death by a gunman. There are riots in black neighborhoods in several cities, including Washington, D.C.

INDEX

205

Index